Guyana Farewell

A RECOLLECTION OF CHILDHOOD IN
A FARAWAY PLACE

by

Noël Compton Bacchus

June 1996
To Wanda:
with my best-wishes
Noël Bacchus

Drawings by Carl Morgan

Acknowledgments

Writing may be, as some have suggested, a solitary occupation. Yet, without the intermittent telephone conversations with my extended family, without the willingness of many to read and respond to segments of the manuscript, without the spontaneous queries of friends that spurred me to resume writing, I doubt whether this book would have been completed. More than any other factor, my sister Sheila's emotional response to the section about my mother, convinced me that I was doing something worthwhile.

I offer my sincere thanks to each of the following and to many others who contributed.

Winnie and Ivan Persaud – for their anecdotes and memories; Gem Eytle – for her prompt help in identifying an illustrator; Emily Deeter – enthusiastic proofreader, ex-officio editor; Camille Lampart – for her assistance, legwork, ideas; Maxey, David and Patrick Bacchus – always ready to listen and to try to remember; Derek Bacchus – for his seemingly effortless translating of ideas into reality; Diane Byam – for her interest and assistance; Elizabeth Rogalin – my editor, for her gentle, knowledgeable suggestions and her nurturing; Joan – my wife, for suggestions, support, tolerance; Norman Gordon – always enthusiastic, always ready to do legwork; Sheila Bacchus Lampart – for her push to publish; Harry Perepeluk – always available to listen and provide help; Robert Kersey – arranging facilities for recording; Felice Rose (Shakespeare Inc.) – for introducing reality to my marketing; Jean Alexander – providing contacts with the Caribbean community in New York; Sybil Chester – source of access to Guyanese and W.I. community; Lisa Lewis and Darlene Van Syckle – enthusiastic and critical readers.

ISBN 0-9624192-1-4

Preface

This book began as an attempt to put into writing the stories of my childhood that I told to my sons, Sebastian and Simon, at bedtime when they were very young. To children born in New York City, growing up far from my own birthplace, these stories must have seemed to them no less magical and fantastic than traditional fairytales.

For me, sitting in the darkness of their room almost 20 years ago, it was the beginning of a long reflection on my formative years that led to insights both painful and revelatory. It involved me in conversations that uncovered feelings and information about those distant days that generated much of the emotion in this chronicle.

I have chosen to use Guyana, the name of the independent country, throughout the book, even though all the events took place during colonial days. For the younger generation the new spelling will be more familiar. For those of my generation it matters little, since it was *home.*

Noel Bacchus

New York City

1995

Christmas Day in the Morning

As faintly as if imagined, the voices trembled in the soft, morning darkness, filtering through a screen of dreams, awakening us to the lovely anticipation of Christmas.

"Oh, little town of Bethlehem,
How still we see thee lie.
Above thy deep and dreamless sleep
The silent stars go by."

Into the pre-dawn stillness of a Guyana morning on Christmas Day came the carolers down the street, singing softly and sweetly of shepherds sleeping and ships a-sailing, of camels and kings, frankincense and myrrh, and of a baby in a manger and a holy night of shining stars. How difficult it is to describe the magical sensation of lying in bed, emerging from a cocoon of dreams to the lovely blend of women's and men's voices lilting through "Jingle Bells," harmonizing softly throughout "Away in a Manger," and rejoicing in "Hark the Herald Angels Sing." My brothers and sister and I would rise quickly, and, as if reluctant to break the spell, steal through the still-dark house silently to the windows and crane our necks to see how soon the carolers would reach our house. The voices drew closer to the quicker tempo of a livelier carol, its joyous refrains dying away to a momentary stillness in which only the sound of a rooster summoning the dawn could be heard. Then, softly, almost imperceptibly, the voices took up the adoring strains of *"O, holy night, the stars are brightly shining…"*

How the custom of caroling on Christmas morning developed in Guyana I do not know, but, as is true for children throughout the world, our holiday traditions seemed as natural to us as breathing. Hanging on the window sills, we listened, enchanted, as the small group sang the familiar carols. The identities of the carolers became clearer little by little as dawn spilled its early light across the

roofs and gardens, grass borders and quiet streets of
Georgetown. We were often delighted to recognize

Guyana Farewell   an elder brother or sister and
perhaps other family friends.

These were not impromptu per-
formances each year, but carefully crafted concerts
evolving from evening rehearsals at our church in
the weeks of December. The voices would rise
and fall in exquisite harmony over the ancient and
familiar melodies, filling the heart with joy and
expectation. The day we had awaited with such
longing had finally arrived.

On Christmas morning – how the phrase
rings in my memory! – the carolers would pause
briefly for some refreshment, perhaps a slice of my
mother's fruitcake and a glass of sorrel or ginger
beer, before assembling once more for a farewell
carol. Their voices faded as they walked away down
the street and around the corner to their next stop.
I REMEMBER LONGING TO GO CAROLING ON CHRIST-
MAS MORNING, to walk the quiet streets before
dawn in the company of friends bringing tidings of
joy to sleeping homes. Yet by the time I was a
young adult these childlike hopes had long yielded

to other dreams and newer aspirations.

As we waited impatiently through the interminable early days of Decem-   *Christmas*
ber, we would be immersed in
a growing swell of preparation
for Christmas. More than anything else connected
to the season, this bustle of preparation excited
and energized us. The adults seemed more intense,
more frantic, more secretive. It was the only time
of the year when so many packages came to our
house. Beneath the bustle of cleaning and polishing, amid the departure and return of newly uphol-
stered couches and re-caned chairs, over and above
the arrival of new linoleum in the kitchen and
the installation of splendidly frilled, new window
curtains, ran a current of expectation that was the
essence of the Christmas season. The small downtown of white-painted, red-roofed, one- and two-
story wooden houses laid out in careful squares and
rectangles twinkled with tiny multi-colored lights
that also trimmed many houses. Christmas trees,
made of wire and green crepe paper in the familiar
cone shape, were festooned with white cotton wool
to simulate snow.

A sure signal of the season's approach was our annual visit to old Mrs. Hunter, the seamstress, to

Guyana Farewell

be measured for new clothes. In her little house a Singer sewing machine was the focus of attention. Bolts of bright cloth, swatches of colorful fabric and reels of vari-colored threads vied for our attention as we were pulled, tugged and assessed with an old tape measure – all the while enduring an incessant stream of queries about schools and friends.

Several afternoons each week, we were expected at our church for rehearsals of the Christmas concert. Our roles might be to sing in a small group, to recite a poem or Bible passage, or to run through the scenes of a play. The prospect of the concert served to temper my growing excitement in anticipation of Christmas. The thought of standing alone on the stage before an expectant congregation produced an immediate stab of apprehension in each of our hearts. Since the concert was held on Christmas evening at our church, all the wonderful events of the holiday were similarly affected – a dark frame to the glowing panorama of the season.

So many of my associations with Christmas are connected to eating and drinking. Not that we were deprived or went hun- *Christmas* gry during the rest of the year, but our family's modest circumstances – that of a minor civil servant, his wife and six children – did not encourage excess. Christmas was the exception. Of course the season was replete with other symbols – twinkling lights and decorations everywhere, wonderful jaunts to the stores on Regent and Water Streets for window shopping, the bustle and frenzy of cleaning and polishing, the appearance of Christmas trees, the radios playing Christmas songs and carols, the churches embellished with scenes recreating the birth of Jesus. YET MY MEMORY IS SUFFUSED WITH THE SMELLS AND TASTES OF THE SPECIAL FOODS OF THE SEASON. For instance, at what point was the Christmas ham delivered? A large imported Smith-field haunch securely encased in a dark, protective covering which had to be carefully cut off – a tradi-tional ritual of preparing the ham for its debut. Eventually the finished product would be displayed in all its brown and pink splendor, studded with cloves, moist with juices, emitting a mouthwatering fragrance.

Guyana Farewell And when did the large red ball of Edam cheese put in its appearance? The brilliant red wrapping had to be removed, disclosing the paler pink of the outer rind of cheese. When the first wedge was carefully cut by my father, disclosing the lovely yellow-gold interior and releasing the Edam's sharp, familiar scent, we could already savor the dry, salty tang of the cheese. HOW WE RELISHED THE THREE-LAYERED BOX OF INDIVIDUALLY WRAPPED CHOCOLATES IN THEIR MULTI-COLORED FOIL, and with what careful deliberation we selected a chocolate from the wonderful array of brightly colored, foil-wrapped morsels, all different sizes and shapes, and how unforgettable the aroma of chocolate and the lovely surprise of the color and flavor within.

There were cellophane packages of dates and figs with their exotic labels, bowls of walnuts, brazil nuts and almond nuts, ornamental tins of Peek Frean biscuits, crisp and pristine in their little compartments. These annual culinary events served to make Christmas special and memorable. It was

the only time of the year that we experienced the
flavor of imported delicacies. We hovered in antici-
pation as our grandfather
unwrapped an "ice apple," an
imported MacIntosh apple,
from its white tissue covering.
After it emerged lusciously
red and succulent, grandfather would slice it and
offer individual wedges to each of us. The fragrance
of those apples, exotic and rare to a boy in Guyana,
stays with me even now.

Christmas was also the season when the special, locally made drinks were available in everyone's
home. One could expect to be offered ginger beer,
mauby – a popular drink made from the bark of a
tree, or fly, a slightly fermented brew from potatoes
– and, most treasured of all when I was a young
child, a bottled orange or grape soda. We might
have delivered to our house a case or two of these
sodas directly from the bottling firms. The open
wooden cases containing a dozen bottles, each with
its colorful label and fizzy soda, were carefully stored
for Christmas Eve, Christmas Day and Boxing Day.
Until as late as 1942 or so, such bottled sodas were

a rare treat. The growing presence of American soldiers at the nearby airbase toward the end of World

War II finally issued in the era
of bottled soda available at every
shop and grocery.

Though Christmas came during the short
rainy season, MY MEMORIES OF THE HOLIDAY ARE OF
DRY, SUNNY DAYS FILLED WITH SOFT, WARM BREEZES
AND FLOWERING, FLAMBOYANT TREES. Perhaps my
love for the season as a boy has lent itself to my
memory of the weather! There were so many special
and intensely awaited events. One of these was that
I was taken downtown to shop for shoes and socks,
whereupon I would have a chance to visit Father
Christmas at one of the two department stores.
How intensely exciting and scary it was to sit on
the knee of this huge, white-bearded, red-suited
person whose voice boomed as he asked if you had
been a good child and what you wanted for Christmas! Another wonderful occurrence was being
given a small amount of money to spend by each
relative. The total might be no more than a few
shillings, but to a child accustomed to begging for
pennies, the prospect of such a sum was heavenly.

A Christmas of Our Own As they had with everything else in our lives, the British put their indelible imprint on our holi-   *Christmas*
days. Or, perhaps, after being created in the image of Britain, we stamped our individuality on the traditions and customs they had bequeathed us. What was the origin of the "masquerade bands" with their drumming, bizarre costumes and masks that both frightened and awed us as children? Why did these bands slowly disappear and give way to the steel bands and calypso singers of later years? Our holidays carried familiar British names – Boxing Day, Old Year's Day, Father Christmas – but beyond those familiar, recognizable names we fashioned unique cultural patterns and customs that distinguished the season. The gaiety and revelry of our Christmas season, with its parties, our enthusiastic sharing of food and drink, our sporting events such as cycle races and boxing matches and, of course, the warmth and sunshine of the tropics – all these made the season uniquely our own in a manner unforgettable.

The voices of the carolers had hardly died

away when the wonderful ritual of opening our presents under the Christmas tree began. Through-

out the visit of the carolers, the youngest ones of the family would be surreptitiously eyeing the gaily wrapped packages and edging slyly in the direction of the tree. Now the gifts could be opened and savored. OUR JOY AT RECEIVING WAS STRONG AND SPONTANEOUS, DESPITE THE QUITE LIMITED NUMBER OF GIFTS WE EXPECTED. In our family of six children, each child received no more than one or two simple gifts. Most attention was lavished on the youngest members of the family.

Small, brightly-painted wind-up cars, a pretty metal box of crayons, a tiny collection of toy soldiers made of lead, a string bag of multicolored glass marbles, packages of two or three white linen or cotton handkerchiefs, a beautiful doll whose blue eyes closed when she was put down in her tiny pram, a painted tin box containing watercolors and a little brush; these and similar modest offerings constituted our cornucopia of joy. Yet I can recollect no sense of disappointment as we showed each other our presents and spent much too short a time

enjoying them before being summoned by my
mother to Christmas breakfast. And what a breakfast! It was a splendid repast *Christmas*
of thick slices of pink ham
with cloves, slivers of Edam
cheese, the familiar aroma of homemade bread –
toasted and slathered with a wonderful, salty
orange-colored butter – hot cocoa for the youngest
and coffee whitened with milk for the older ones.
Inspired by the special abundance of Christmas
morning's breakfast and our joy about our presents,
we bounced and bubbled and chattered irrepress-
ibly in an atmosphere freed of the usual quiet and
restrained manner of other mornings.

We were allowed an hour or two of respite on
Christmas morning to play with our gifts or read a
new book of Grimm's *Fairy Tales* or engage in a
board game, such as Snakes and Ladders. My father
indulgently presided, listening to a church service on
the radio or to the Christmas songs and carols while
my mother and the maid made the beds, washed up
the dishes and straightened the house before the latter could leave for their homes and Christmases.
Soon it would be time to go to our grandmother's

house for the traditional Christmas meal.

To sit in a moment of quiet play with a new

Guyana Farewell toy on Christmas day, with the voices of my brothers nearby, my sister perhaps running through scales on the piano, my father tuning in the radio to the holiday music, was to be suspended in an intense sense of happiness that became rarer as I grew older and finally vanished forever from my life. I HAVE BEEN HAPPY MANY TIMES SINCE BUT NO LONGER WITH THAT PURE, UNADULTERATED BLISSFULNESS OF EARLY CHILDHOOD IN THE BOSOM OF MY FAMILY. Perhaps it was the relaxed and calmer demeanor of my mother or maybe it was the exceptionally indulgent manner of my father, but an unfamiliar serenity and goodwill filled the house and a feeling of happy excitement and expectation pervaded all activities on Christmas day. Whatever the reason, everything seemed brighter, more promising, more hopeful. I believe my whole family felt that way, but we never spoke of it.

My grandparent's home symbolised Christmas for us. They lived two blocks down the street and we went there every Christmas for lunch.

Arriving there on Christmas Day, we would
be greeted by the wonderfully potent aroma of
grandfather's rum swizzle. A *Christmas*
delectable concoction of
milk, eggs, sugar and dark,
fragrant Demerara rum, the heady scent and the
intoxicating sound of swizzle sticks being deftly
manipulated by Grandfather immediately put the
stamp of authenticity on Christmas Day. Hoping
for a small sip of this magical potion, I would hurry
ahead of mother, always trying to get there before
she arrived so that Grandfather, with a gleam in his
eye, might offer a tiny glass containing a splash of
the pale, golden-brown, foamy-cold deliciously different treat. Careful to wipe any betraying evidence
from my lips, I would wait apprehensively to hear
mother's denunciation of my grandfather's indulgence in strong liquor. She would castigate him,
citing appropriate biblical passages while brushing
off his sheepish, feeble protestations of her right-
cousness. My grandmother, with her hands akimbo,
might emerge from the dining room to survey
this scene and add her skeptical assessment of the
behavior of her daughter.

In the dining room, a large, polished mahogany table covered with an intricately embroidered

tablecloth, would be set for
twelve on Christmas day.

Nearby was a smaller table for
the younger children. Through the door of the
kitchen, one of Granny's two servants could usually
be seen putting finishing touches to the platters
of fried plantains and sweet potatoes, a tureen of
soup, large dishes of pigeon peas or black-eyed peas
and rice, the golden, brown distended breast of the
turkey, shining with its basting of oil and gravy, the
roasted potatoes and baked pigeons. BEST OF ALL
WAS THE RICH DARK-BROWN STUFFING WITH ITS
WONDERFUL FRAGRANCE OF SPICE AND HERBS, baked
and simmered and nurtured through the previous
day and evening until the air was heavy and redo-
lent with its residue. The soft tropical breeze that
stirred the curtains served only to waft the delicious
odors back and forth. They filled my senses and
tantalized my appetite.

My uncles and aunts would emerge from
upstairs with smiles and greetings. All was laughter
and banter and teasing remarks with warm hugs.

During all this, my mother would be uncharacteristically inactive, acknowledging the greetings of her family with a solemn, almost *Christmas* uncomfortable reserve. It was as if such demonstrativeness was inappropriate in her opinion. My father, meanwhile, exhibited the smiling, cordial manner, always evident in his encounters with family and friends. It was at times like this that we could see beyond the serious, occasionally forbidding presence he maintained at home, to what must have been a charming, vivacious young man in his earlier days.

Christmas night and the inevitable, and dreaded, church concert would finally come. Every pew in the plain white wooden church would be filled with church members, parents and visitors. Christmas decorations of suitably biblical tradition were enhanced by bouquets of flowers. Mingled scents of powder, perfume and sweat were wafted back and forth by the many hand-held fans. The concert program would be carefully examined for the names of participating relatives. The turning of its pages, added to the soft murmur of subdued voices and the rustle of starched shirts and pinafores, taffeta

and tulle, created a rising, expectant sound that
drifted to where the performers, all children, sat in

varying degrees of nervous
anticipation. Crowded together
with the group on the small
wooden benches in the front of the church, itchy
from the starch in my long-sleeved blue shirt,
I would concentrate on admiring my new patent
leather shoes and try not to fiddle with my tie.
I remember the aroma of Beck's brilliantine with
which my hair was slicked, of coconut oil from
someone else's hair and the ever-present fragrance
of Yardley's face powder with which all our faces
were dusted.

What a sigh of pleasure and appreciation
greeted a particularly polished performance – an
impeccable curtsey and the faultless recitation of a
passage from the Psalms, a smart salute and the
rendition of a familiar poem. Equally appreciated,
though tempered by carefully moderated amusement, might be a less perfect offering, perhaps
assisted by an audible prompting from backstage
until the child had successfully completed her performance. And, of course, the occasional performer,

paralyzed by stagefright when confronted by the sea of faces, retreated in confusion after interminable moments of painful silence as *Christmas* the congregation radiated sympathy and encouragement.

How I hated it all! Sitting, mutinously impassive, resentful of my companions' eager participation, I waited to recite or sing or take part in a small pageant. I WAS ALWAYS CERTAIN THAT I WOULD FORGET MY LINES, MISS MY CUE, AND APPEAR RIDICULOUS. I don't recall ever doing so, but the expectation of it was enough. I did not understand then and still do not comprehend the adults' need for this type of forced affirmation.

Boxing Day Freedom   Boxing Day, the day after Christmas, was a public holiday, and it was imbued with an exhilarating sense of freedom for us. We were free of the religious rituals of Christmas, free of the family obligations of visits and gifts, and everyone pursued their particular favorite pastime. All of the social clubs organized dances (as officially organized parties with admission fees were called) that began in the early afternoon and went on into the evening. Music was supplied by

orchestras or steelbands and the open bars flowed
with rum and mixers of ginger ale, soda and coke.

Guyana Farewell Shandy, a mixture of beer
and lemonade, another British
acquisition, was a popular
option. The rum shops were filled with noisy
drunken carousers. Organized bicycle races and
goat races were held in many public parks. More
surreptitiously, dog fights and cockfights took place
in concealed backyards and alleyways.

For me, awakening on Boxing Day brought
the joy of relief that the Christmas concert was
behind me and I could play uninterrupted with my
new toys, show them to my friends, admire theirs.
I could roam the neighborhood at will, play cricket
or football, race bicycles or run footraces. It was
one of the few days of the year that could be devoted solely to pleasure. In every home, visitors
stopped by for lively conversations, sampled the
rum-flavored Christmas fruit cake and ginger beer,
dropped off late gifts. Everywhere radios played
popular songs or the records spun endlessly on the
gramophones. The billboards around town were
usually plastered with huge posters about prize

fights, dances, concerts and entertainments of every sort that would take place during the period until New Year's Day. Rain fre- *Christmas* quently necessitated the post- poning or curtailing of some of the outdoor activities, but did little to dampen the revelry. Bicyclists in singles, pairs and groups, talking and laughing loudly hurried to parties, sporting activities and other pursuits.

For Auld Lang Syne, My Dear... Old Year's Day and evening were the domain of adults. I recall the slightly forlorn feeling I experienced as I observed my aunts and uncles making preparations for an evening of festivities. But even so, a feeling of excitement and expectation permeated the late afternoon and evening. The sports clubs and dance halls were festooned with brightly colored garlands of crepe paper, while balloons in bunches swayed and bumped, and dance bands and orchestras could be heard rehearsing. Radios everywhere played sentimental favorites with lines like, "Now is the hour when we must say goodbye" or "Oh, how we danced on the night we were wed" and, of course, "Auld Lang Syne." The very air seemed to anticipate both the bittersweet recollection of the dying year and the toasts and revelry that would greet the *Guyana Farewell* new. At the many Catholic churches, midnight mass was popular and our close friends who lived nearby considered it a command occasion. Struggling and usually failing to stay awake, I might drift off to the faint sounds of an orchestra at the dance hall two blocks away and awaken momentarily to churchbells at midnight ringing out the old and welcoming the new year.

On New Year's morning, quiet pervaded our town. Except for an occasional pair of revellers cycling tipsily home, the streets would rest silently under the bright sunshine of a tropical morning, the faint breeze from the sea tossing a wayward balloon or blowing a residue of confetti across the empty streets.

Mother: A Force of Nature

I often remember my mother convulsed with laughter, so overcome by and helpless in the grasp of whatever had precipitated her amusement that tears ran from her eyes which she mopped, embarrassed, with the back of her hand.

In this particular memory, she sits at our dining table long ago, and her round face is contorted with her efforts to restrain what she felt was a wayward sense of humor. At that moment I had a glimpse of the lively, carefree child my Aunt May would tell me about much later, far from Guyana.

That this should be such a vivid memory for me is ironic, because no one who knew my mother would have characterized her as frivolous. In repose, her demeanor was grave, almost impassive, often stern. Such repose was, however, equally uncharacteristic. SHE SEEMED TO DEFINE HERSELF BY DETERMINED ACTIVITY FROM EARLIEST MORNING TO LATE AT NIGHT. So much of my mother's activity and energy had to do with her intense religious fervor.

The eldest of six children, born to a civil servant, Herbert Grannum, and his wife, Anita, Mother was not much over five feet tall, sturdily built, with a light brown complexion and a pretty, round face. In her teenage years and early twenties, she was, according to her close friends, one of a carefree and vivacious group that partied, danced and enjoyed life. She met my father, Hassan Bacchus, at the office of the Registrar of Deeds where they both worked. I know little of the early years of their marriage but an event took place, perhaps seven years later, that changed their lives dramatically.

At the age of 28, my mother was "saved" and converted to a devout Christian life in the form of an American fundamentalist sect named Pilgrim Holiness. The missionaries of this sect traveled throughout the world from their headquarters in Indianapolis, Indiana to spread the word of God.

Exotic in their wholesomeness and surprisingly –
genuinely – warm and generous, these Americans

Guyana Farewell were notably different from
the resident British in their lack
of affectation. What was not
surprising was that their hymn-singing, hand-clap-
ping, pulpit-pounding type of religion captivated
an element of the populace previously constrained
by the bloodless strictures of the Anglican church
and the trappings of a Victorian society. The irony
of the conversion was that it released the energy
and exuberance of the converts to sing and praise
the Lord vigorously, at the same time that it
engulfed them in a new series of constraints – long
dresses and long sleeves, forbidden ornamentation,
unacknowledged sexuality and unending restrictions. NO DANCING, NO ALCOHOL, NO SMOKING, NO
JEWELRY, NO PARTIES. ("NO NOTHING," WE USED TO
SAY AS CHILDREN.)

On awakening, my mother would spend as
much as fifteen minutes kneeling at her bedside, in
silent prayer. Every morning, all of us were summoned to family prayers by the sound of my mother playing the piano as she sang a hymn. Only my

father was exempt from this ritual. His parents were
Muslims and, although he only occasionally went
to the mosque, he declined to   *Mother: A Force*
participate. Yet, even he was   *of Nature*
eventually worn down as the
years went by. Family prayers consisted of reading
one chapter from the King James Bible, followed by
my mother's praying aloud as we all kneeled, eyes
closed. We read completely through the Bible, Old
Testament and New, Genesis to Revelations, only
to begin all over again at "In the beginning God
created the heaven and the earth...." Each of us,
from the time we were old enough to repeat the
words of whoever was holding us on their lap, read
a verse in turn, going around the circle. We were
excruciatingly bored by the "begats," as in: "And
Peleg lived thirty years and begat Reu..."; rendered
incredulous by, "And Shem lived after he begat
Arphaxad five hundred years and begat sons and
daughters..."; enormously titillated as teenagers,
when Abram "went in unto Hagar and she con-
ceived..."; and we were thrilled and mesmerized by
David and Jonathan, Samson and Delilah, Sodom
and Gomorra. Throughout our early childhoods

and young adolescence and, finally, our rebellious teen years, we were enveloped in a fog of doctrine,

myth, salvation and always, ominously, the threat of hellfire and damnation for all eternity.

The Holy Bible defined the lives of those, like my mother, who had been converted, in levees of quoted scriptures. There were biblical allusions for every occasion. There were verses to chastise by and threaten with, passages to pontificate from, and an endless suffocation of sentiments praising, exhorting, cautioning, inspiring and damning its converts and those beyond the pale. My mother possessed an encyclopedic knowledge of the Bible. She could deliver projectiles of opprobrium, showers of approbation, barrages of reproof, thunderbolts of condemnation, and all were couched in appropriate biblical language. Not for her the simple bromides familiar to any casual Bible student. Even the strait-jacket of piety could not repress her natural need to excel. OBSCURE YET PITHY REFERENCES SPRINKLED HER DISCOURSE. Her rebukes, enunciated carefully and delivered in ominous rolling cadences, would have done justice to Jeremiah, and often did. "Woe to the rebellious children, saith the Lord," she intoned, in response to some breach of conduct or neglect of obligation and duty. She owed much to the prophet Isaiah, comfortably

Mother: A Force of Nature

assuming his mantle, using the enormous range of his utterances to praise, threaten, castigate and smite her audiences. None escaped her vigilance. Not my grandfather, her father, who submitted to her reprovals with a wry, baffled astonishment which seemed to imply, "Did I sire this child?" Nor did her mother, my grandmother, escape, who responded indignantly to being lectured or admonished for her maliciousness; not her sisters and brothers, whose frivolousness and pursuit of 'worldly goods' inspired her biting condemnation. Not a member of our community whose iniquitous behavior may have come to her attention.

Her favorite denunciations seemed to have a rhythm and balance that was hypnotic. "The heart is deceitful above all things and desperately wicked; who can know it." "Wine is a mocker, strong drink is raging: and whosoever is deceived thereby is not wise." Whereas in other people this type of pontifi-

cation would seem theatrical, my mother would
speak these baroque phrases in a manner so natural

Guyana Farewell   that it only served to define
and accentuate the strength of
her personality.

My mother's given name was Vivian and at
some point in her life, she came to be known as
Sister V. Whether this was the result of her church
where all in their congregation were referred to as
Brother "this" and Sister "that," or whether from
some other incident, many who knew her, regard-
less of their own affiliations, addressed her thus.
In most cases it was affectionate, but always tempered with other sentiments: respect, apprehension,
resentment, amusement and often, awe. She seemed
a force of nature – focused, implacable, unbending.

As an aspiring poet in my teenage years, I
developed the daunting suspicion that my mother's
seemingly excessive recourse to the Psalms might
possibly be inspired by sheer pleasure. Listening to
her intone passages from the Song of Solomon sent
tremors of recognition through me.

"I am black, but comely, O ye daughters of
Jerusalem, as the tents of Kedar, as the curtains of

Solomon." "Stay me with flagons, comfort me with apples: for I am sick of love." Her voice at morning prayers would sing on the stanzas: "For lo, the winter is past, the rain is over and gone; the flowers appear on the earth; the time of the singing of the birds is come,

Mother: A Force of Nature

and the voice of the turtle is heard in the land."

That this elemental force, this strong, plainly-attired, domineering person who could chastise vocally or punish physically; this woman who railed against vanity, condemned the use of alcohol, jewelry, immodest clothing, dancing and revelry, pop music and all movies, might derive pleasure from the bright refrains and dark rhythms of Solomon, distill sweetness from the dense, powerful declarations of Jeremiah, find favor with the fabric woven of magic and myth of Judges and Kings, was disturbing to contemplate. This idea, like others I briefly entertained as a child, I dismissed as too fanciful and disconcerting to consider seriously. Yet, to hear her declaim in a voice momentarily muted and hesitant:

"How shall we sing the Lord's song in a strange land? If I forget thee, O Jerusalem, let my

Guyana Farewell   right hand forget her cunning." Or to sense intimations of joy and to suspect pleasure as she seemed to dwell on some passages, was an echo pursuing my consciousness as we knelt in prayer those distant mornings.

My mother seldom allowed her religious pursuits to prevent her from fulfilling her familial responsibilities. In a society where most women assumed the traditional roles of mother and home-maker after marriage, she was not satisfied with a passive exercise of those duties. The needs of a growing family, (eventually five boys and one girl), exceeded the resources of my father's meager salary, who was a civil servant. HER EXPECTATIONS FOR US WERE COUPLED WITH HER DETERMINATION TO PRO-VIDE THE OPPORTUNITIES TO FULFILL THOSE SAME EXPECTATIONS. Money was needed to pay for music lessons, for academic tutoring in pursuit of scholar-ships, and to permit eventual overseas study. She proceeded to generate the required additional income in a variety of ways. At the same time she established a strict, impossible-to-escape, futile-to-resist regimen for us of school work, music lessons, special tutoring and chores. *Mother: A Force of Nature*

Exactly when she began making jams and jellies for sale, I don't recall. What is certain is that she made a trip to the U.S.A. in 1930, under the sponsorship of the American missionaries at her church. This trip expanded her horizons enormously, triggering a latent entrepreneurial force in her personality. Visits to farming families in Indiana and Illinois enabled her to observe and learn the processes of canning and preserving fruit and involved her in the efficiency and energy of rural American domestic life. This was a vastly different experience from the carefully structured, stylized constraints of life in a small colonial society.

By the time I became conscious of the significance of her enterprises, my mother's work had already achieved the size of a cottage industry. She was generating hundreds of jars of guava jelly neatly packaged in screw top glass jars, and attractively identified by a colorful printed label. When the crop of guavas was low or the season ended, she would switch to a variety of alternative preserves, made from less abundant or lesser known fruits – pineapple jam, Seville orange marmalade, cherry jam – and even manufactured peanut butter that was as popular with us as it was with her many satisfied customers.

Guyana Farewell

During the periods of my mother's greatest production, the kitchen of our home was a simmer of boiling vessels and crackling coal pots. The rhythmic "thwok thwok" of wood being chopped in the bottom house was often our first waking sound. A cast iron stove fueled with wood and several coal pots with charcoal were lit as early as 5 a.m. and constantly replenished throughout the day. These kept large pots of water boiling, into which the heaps of quartered guavas were shoveled. Vendors from the markets arrived with large baskets of guavas on their heads – contracted for by my mother on the previous day. If the vendors failed to appear, my mother would not hesitate to get on her bicycle, ride to the market and engage in stern bargaining.

"Look a dese guavas, missus. Dey ripe an' sweet! Ah gun give yuh a good price," came the pleas. To

which my mother might respond:

"Those too green," or, *"Half a' them almost rotten."* *"Ah gun pick out de* Mother: A Force of Nature *bes' ones fuh yuh, mum."*

Successful, she returned home with laden baskets hanging on the handles of her bicycle. I remember how she used to maneuver her bike with its heavy load across the little wooden bridge in front of our house, through our small gate and into our yard, and descend with a little skipping run. Fortunately, her children inherited her agility and athletic skill! Meanwhile, Ivy or Ada or one of the many women she employed, had been busily stoking the stoves, quartering guavas, adding ingredients to the boiling pots. Sweating in the heat, they would talk and sing and complain, with an occasional apprehensive aside to each other:

"Yuh bettah stop drinkin' dat tea an' finish dem bottles! Sister V. gun fix yuh propah!"

My mother's return was similar to a small hurricane. A furiously ringing bicycle bell, a rattle of wooden boards on the bridge, a clatter of a too-loose bicycle chain was followed by her peremptory call from downstairs, summoning the nearest person to assist her in unloading her cargo.

"Ada?! ....Ivy?! ... One 'a you, come quick!"

Woe to those passersby in front of our house, caught in the wake of her urgent requirements!

"You, fella! Yes! You! Come here and help me!"

Unceremoniously drafted to carry heavy baskets of fruit up the stairs or to help unload an enormous bag of sugar from the donkey cart that had just arrived, or to assist in lugging bags of charcoal or loads of firewood from the storeroom, HE WOULD BE COAXED AND CAJOLED, PRAISED OR ADMONISHED and finally sent on his way, clutching a bottle of guava jelly and a few Bible tracts, mumbling incoherently about bossy females.

"Da woman mus' be crazy! Dem bags too heavy fah she. Wha' is dis she gimme? She mus' tink I sum muscle boy!"

All morning, my mother and the two servants ceaselessly quartered guavas, replenished boiling pots, stoked stoves, and poured hot, liquid jelly, and by mid-afternoon, scores of jars of jelly cooled in shallow pans of water. Meanwhile, they had cooked the main meal of the day, to be consumed by six hungry children and her husband at midday.

Most afternoons during her busy season of producing preserves, my mother, satisfied with the progress achieved that day,

Mother: A Force of Nature

would set out on her bicycle to attend to the many administrative details of her enterprises. These might include delivering a couple of dozen jars of jelly to a customer, negotiating a sale or establishing a contract for a future delivery, persuading a store to display her product more centrally, arranging for the next day's supply of fruit by a vendor, or 100-lb bags of sugar or charcoal by the owner of a donkey cart, or presenting carefully handwritten invoices for payment. Whenever we were available during school breaks, vacations or weekends, we were pressed into assuming some of these duties. We delivered goods on our bicycles, collected payments, pasted labels on bottles, quartered guavas, shelled peanuts, brought buckets of water or loads of firewood up the back stairs and were required to remain within earshot for requests of further duty.

Except for one incident that marked me irrevocably, we considered these duties my mother pressed upon us an inescapable, if annoying, intrusion by adults into our lives. Though the details of

Guyana Farewell

the incident are not clear in my memory, my emotional reaction is still with me today. My mother, accompanied by me, had made a delivery at one of the larger stores, which was owned by a white merchant, either Portuguese or British. He instructed my mother brusquely to present the invoice in the business office upstairs. Sweaty and somewhat disheveled from our bicycle ride in the hot sun and the exertion of unloading the goods from our bicycles, she went to the office with me in tow. I can still remember the sense of shame and anger I experienced at the deprecatory manner of the office manager as he received, scrutinized and finally paid the bill as we waited. My mother's composure and stern serenity appeared impervious to his attitude, but I seethed with resentment. I often wondered since: how accurate is that recollection? Was it my adolescent resentment of being dragged along on an errand by a parent? Or was I sensing, even at that age, resentment of a woman's intrusion into a traditionally male sphere of activity?

Nothing could inflame my mother more quickly than to utter a summons to one of us on a busy day and have it go unheeded. She would then descend on us like a thunder *Mother: A Force of Nature* bolt. Though sturdily built, she was light on her feet and quick. With a short leather strap in hand, she summarily terminated whatever game or pastime we were engaged in. Whoever was nearest or most preoccupied would feel the weight of her arm, and the frenzied scattering and shouts of alarm and pain as we fled her wrath would give way to our laughter and mockery of those who were victims. Nevertheless, as soon as we considered it safe, we would sidle into the house and present ourselves for duty. Occasionally my mother's anger and exertions would yield to her sense of the ridiculous and she would return to the kitchen panting and laughing, much to the surprise of her helpers.

Father

Remote yet omnipresent, outwardly calm yet easily exasperated, quiet yet capable of explosive rage, my father was the most enigmatic presence in my life as a child. Small, trim, self-contained and always impeccably dressed, his presence was both unobtrusive and constant. Mostly silent when he was home, my father's comments were usually directed at the shortcomings of his sons, his wife or the household staff. I do not recall any criticism of my sister. Neatness, order and routine were vitally important to him and he duly noted and addressed any transgressions irritably or angrily.

In retrospect, I understand why my father was prone to explosions of temper now and then. Here was this quiet, self-possessed man living in our small house with its three tiny bedrooms, six active, athletic children and a powerful, constantly on-the-move wife. Occasionally, the sense of being hemmed in and jostled must have seemed sufficiently overwhelming that only by expressing anger could he cope with the situation.

His physical space comprised no more than his half of a bed shared with his youngest child, in a bedroom that contained a second double bed shared by two other sons. A towel rack and two hooks behind a door, together with a small shelf, sufficed for all his everyday articles – pajamas, underwear, and shaving and grooming requirements. A SINGLE WARDROBE IN THE CORNER OF THE ADJOINING BEDROOM CONTAINING HIS SUITS AND OTHER POSSESSIONS WAS SHARED WITH HIS FIVE SONS. The top of a bureau, covered with a heavy cloth, served as an ironing board. Every morning wrinkles were ironed out of shirts and pleats in trousers were carefully restored.

My father's daily ritual of meticulous preparations – carefully brushing his shoes to a satisfactory gloss, testing the iron with a careful finger before

pressing his shirt, combing and brushing his hair
to the exact neatness required for his satisfaction,

securing his tie with a compact,
perfect Windsor knot – all these
were observed and unconscious-
ly emulated by his children. As a result, a neater,
cleaner, more fastidious group is difficult to conceive of. ONE OF THE FEW PHOTOGRAPHS OF US AS
CHILDREN THAT I POSSESS FULLY ILLUSTRATES OUR
PASSION FOR ORDER, NEATNESS AND CONTROL. Even
the youngest of the group, my brother Maxey, a
child of no more than two years, is neat and clean,
with carefully brushed hair and an intent, serious
countenance that matches those of his siblings.

All of my father's activities were carefully
orchestrated and unchanging throughout his life.
His morning meal of toast, tea, and a boiled egg
was always prepared and checked by my mother
or a servant – the slightest variation or mistake in
preparation was enough to make him irritable and
petulant. His departure for work each weekday
and Saturday morning were similarly ritualized.
Impeccably attired in a white or tan suit, he would
pause for a few minutes downstairs in the yard

beneath our house, stand next to his bicycle, and
smoke a cigarette. Tossing the half-smoked cigarette
away, he would walk his bicy-   *Father*
cle out through the rear gate,
past the wide grass verge to
the roadway, mount up, and ride off with erect posture, one hand holding the bicycle handle, the
other setting his gray or brown felt hat firmly on his
head. I have an enduring picture in my mind of the
days when my youngest brother, Maxey, traveled to
school first on the crossbar of Daddy's bicycle and,
later, rode his own small bike alongside my father's.
The amusing juxtaposition of my father's slow,
stately progression of pedals and Maxey's rapidly
churning legs was an endearing sight.

As regular as his departure, so was my father's
return home every weekday afternoon between 5:30
and 6:00 p.m. Cycling in a more leisurely fashion,
occasionally even holding his hat in one hand,
he would more often than not ride over our little
wooden bridge directly into the yard beneath the
house before dismounting from his bicycle.

My father's evening activities were as predictable as all his other routines. Retiring to the

bedroom, he would remove and hang up all of his clothes carefully, then don his pajamas and slippers

before taking his supper. Unlike morning tea, when he would usually be joined by whichever of us had finished getting ready for school, he often ate by himself in the evening. His supper was prepared and left by the servant or my mother. AFTER SUPPER, HE WOULD CAREFULLY WASH THE DISHES and then either listen to the radio or sit in the gallery overlooking the street and watch the passing scene. He went to bed fairly early – not much after the youngest child, who, as mentioned, shared a double bed with him. I have no recollection of my father ever sharing a bed with my mother.

I only slowly became aware of my father's interest in our athletic accomplishments as children. This was in part because our athletic activities during our elementary years were confined to schoolyard and street games. It was not until secondary school that we had a chance to participate in any sort of organized sports. This new opportunity was so wonderful that we all tended to be intensely preoccupied with the tryouts for various teams, the frenzied speculation about whether we would see our name posted on the team rosters for cricket, field hockey or soc- *Father* cer. Then, provided we were selected for the team, we became so intent on performing well in practice games that we neither cared nor noticed anyone's interest other than that of our peers.

By the second year, when we began to take our participation in sports more for granted, we became interested in the quality of our equipment, which was normally supplied by the school. If you became accomplished, you wanted to have your own. This would probably be a hand-me-down from an elder brother. Eventually and more happily, it would be replaced by one's own new cricket bat.

I don't recall the first time I noticed Daddy watching one of us play in a formal league game, but I recall distinctly my surprise and dawning pleasure. It meant that he had altered his regular activities and made a special effort to get there in time, a consideration I found as interesting as it was touching. It may have been the first time that I ever saw my father as human instead of a symbol or overarching presence. Once I became aware of him as a person, I found myself thinking about him and

his preoccupations every once in a while. I recall clearly, at some point in my teenage years, observing my father in one of his regular spots, sitting on the arm of a chair by the window, looking out into the street. I wondered what he was thinking about, and I surmised that since he was so often physically inactive, the life of his mind must be considerable and continuous. As I watched him in repose, there was a stillness and to me, a sadness, about his posture that was as disconcerting as it may have been fanciful.

One of the most vivid memories I have of my father is a Christmas meal at my grandparent's house. My eldest brother, Pat, had left home earlier in the year to attend college in North America. We were about to sit down for our meal when the telephone rang. Uncle John bounded up the short flight of stairs to the small landing where the telephone box hung on the wall. It was Pat, calling on his first Christmas Day away from the family. In 1948 such a call took a long time to place and was very expensive, so there was only time for a brief exchange of greetings. As I recall, only my parents and grandfather spoke to my brother. My father, on the strong urging of my grand-mother (with whom he had an almost filial relationship),

Father

took the receiver reluctantly and, it seemed, at the first sound of my brother's voice, broke into tears and began to sob loudly. Someone, perhaps my mother or Uncle John, finally took the phone from him and resumed the exchange of greetings. I sat in consternation trying to sort out my feelings as I watched various members of the family offering sympathy and comfort to my father. The meal passed in something of a daze. I have never forgotten the vision of my weeping father with all its implications of parental love and loss.

The child that was me sat solemnly watching this scene, shocked out of his normally quiet, introverted demeanor, trying to make sense of his father's grief, trying to reconcile this weeping, vulnerable person with the stern, mostly reserved, occasionally angry and violent man that until that moment had been an essential image in that little boy's life.

Guyana Farewell   With no one to confide in, I must have internalized the event, absorbed the shock and, in what was to become a common pattern, reviewed the matter interminably until I found myself able to absorb its impact and relegate it to some compartment of my memory. I have little recollection of what my mother was doing during all this, but I can remember my grandmother trying to comfort my father with pats and gentle ridicule. Around us the fragrant heat from our meal rose, the sounds of carols and sermons on radios in neighboring houses drifted in, accustomed events occurred. My world had slipped sideways unmistakably and unforgettably.

I never achieved anything like a genuine emotional relationship with my father. OURS WAS A RELATIONSHIP THAT MIXED RESPECT WITH RESIS-TANCE, AFFECTION WITH RESENTMENT. After I left home to go overseas, there were times when I was afflicted by the sense that I could have done more to show him my love. Once, on a train going from

Tokyo to Osaka, I turned my head and saw a reflection in the windowpane that for a fleeting moment seemed to be my father. The *Father* rush of emotion was instant. The recognition that it was my own reflection, was disconcerting and disorienting. I sat there sadly, surrounded by strangers, needing comfort, once more a child.

As I grew older I became increasingly reconciled that what I could not change I should not agonize about. It is enough that I remember him now with affection and appreciation. As a child, I was so overwhelmed by his simple presence that I never really knew how much he loved and cherished us all.

As the years went by, we inadvertently discovered his fierce pride in our activities and accomplishments, but rarely because of any word of praise or forthright acknowledgment of a triumph. When we were capable of stepping outside of the intense preoccupation with self that is childhood, we could see that this father, this slightly mocking, amused presence, this source of cricket bats and hockey sticks, soccer boots and spiked running shoes, bicycle pumps and shoe brushes, might actually love you and be proud of your success on the athletic

Guyana Farewell
field and in the academic forum. This seemingly impervious presence might bristle at any apparent slight to your performance, or he might bloom with pleasure when he was complimented by others on your achievements.

As children, my siblings and I never questioned – in fact, rarely contemplated – the nature of our father's activities. The predictability of his presence, arrivals and departures, the regularity of his behavior and the unchanging character of his daily and weekly regimen were to us as unconsciously reassuring as the seasons. My father's routines were inestimable in their value to our sense of security, but no more recognized or acknowledged than the roof of our house. Where my mother had to exhort, scold, push, bully, chastise, manage and administer, my father was able to maintain an authority in both his presence and absence that was rarely challenged. Because she was always interacting with us, my mother aroused emotional reaction – anger, admiration, amusement, resentment, embarrassment – but never indifference.

My father's work at the Law Courts, his office, and his colleagues were mysteri- *Father* ous to us, but of obvious importance. On the few occa- sions, as we grew older, when we had reason to visit him at his office on the ground floor of the elegant Victorian building at the corner of South Road and High Street, WE STOOD AWKWARDLY AND SHYLY AS HE BRIEFLY INTRODUCED US TO HIS STAFF. We were tongue-tied by the strangeness of the occa- sion and the affability of this smiling, unfamiliar, shirt-sleeved person held in obvious esteem by his colleagues and associates.

After he completed high school, my father went to work as an office boy at the Law Courts. From this beginning he worked his way steadily upwards in the Civil Service to the position of Registrar of Deeds. Close to the time of his retire- ment, he was awarded an M.B.E. (Member of the British Empire) at the annual ceremonies celebrated throughout the Empire and Commonwealth on the occasion of the monarch's birthday. This constitut- ed the peak of his career.

When I look at the photograph I have of him
standing erect, proudly serious as the ribbon is

Guyana Farewell   pinned to his lapel by the Chief
Justice, it reminds me of the
Empire Day parades when the
British anthem was playing, when the military
bands and colorful horse guards marched in front
of admiring crowds, and the Union Jack fluttered
in the breeze to the sound of crisp commands and
marching feet.

Civil Service salaries were not considerable,
so it is baffling to understand how my father managed to support a family of eight, provide us with
all the accoutrements for school, athletic activities,
toys and games, and even put away money in
his Building Society savings plan for emergencies.
Naturally thrifty, abstemious in his personal behavior, careful with all his belongings, he differed from
my mother so dramatically that only the attraction
of opposites can possibly explain their relationship.

Rains Came

Intensely humid and hot weeks preceded the coming of the rains. I recall my father plucking his shirt away from his sticky shoulders as the sun scorched down from cloudless, blue skies.

The still air, unrelieved by any breeze, rested like heavy flannel on our exposed skin. My father would exclaim irritably about the persistence of the heat and long for a cool breeze. Yet, when it arrived, its cool dampness a relief for some, the rainy season was a mixed blessing.

Rain altered the rhythms of life. Everything became sodden: wet shoes stuffed with newspapers; wet clothes hanging on lines in the kitchen at night; wet bicycle saddles and backsides; wet trees and soccer fields (empty due to canceled games); wet people huddled under trees, awnings or dripping canopies that occasionally collapsed; sodden stalls of fruits and vegetables palely gleaming in the open air markets, presided over by vendors under huge, black, mostly broken umbrellas.

There was a short rainy season and a long one. Huge banks of black, threatening clouds heralded the arrival of these seasons. Silver-gray curtains of rain advanced down streets, enveloping the quietly huddling houses and fences and gardens.

LARGE, BLACK AND UNWIELDY, UMBRELLAS BLOOMED LIKE SUDDEN DARK FLOWERS EVERYWHERE. They caused altercations and parental exasperation – broken umbrellas, missing umbrellas, insufficient umbrellas! In a family of eight, even when umbrellas could be afforded, someone would always be lending or losing or breaking one; the reliable ones were likely to be reserved for parents, while others were distributed willy-nilly.

On rainy mornings, flotillas of bicycles with black umbrellas unfurling like unwieldy sails, filled the streets of our town. Bicycle bells ringing and tires peeling off wet streets were a discordant intru-

sion in the normally hushed gray morning air. The
hubbub of umbrella-induced altercations disturbed
Guyana Farewell   the tranquillity of houses and
                          gardens, of cricket grounds and
                          graveyards crouched under the
slow drip-dripping of mango trees and coconut
palms, amid the faint scent of roses and the damp
glow of hibiscus and bougainvillea.

In the rainy season, the zinc sheeting on the
roof of our house reverberated with drumming
raindrops. All night long, snug in our beds, lulled
by the rattle of rain on roofs and windowpanes, WE
DREAMT OF SOURSOP AND SORREL, PATTIES AND
PALOWRI, HOLIDAYS AND HAMMOCKS. Some nights
we were roused from sleep by my father's voice
exhorting us to help move the bed away from a leak
in the roof, or we woke to see him positioning a
pan to catch water from a dripping eave. Thunder
cracked loudly throughout the night.

We awoke to gray, cool mornings, the
overnight clamor reduced to a murmuring drizzle.
We had to be coaxed from our beds during the
rainy season when the days were markedly cooler
and our beds, snug and warm. We were reluctant to

take our turn in the shower, which was the only way to bathe in most homes.

The shower was in a small enclosed space in the kitchen, open at the top, with a concrete floor and a drain. There was a raised wooden platform with slats to stand on. The cold water flowing from a large shower head, straight down over our warm children's bodies, was sheer torture most mornings. Our house reverberated with our shrieks as we dashed into the water, flailing furiously at ourselves with soap while jumping up and down.

These morning showers were strictly regulated in both time and sequence – six children needed to rise, shower, dress, have prayers, breakfast and leave for school by 8 a.m. Anything that jeopardized the schedule or anyone who overslept would rue the day. Rousted by exasperated siblings, accompanied by whacks from Mother's heavy hand, we would be hurried into the shower, stunned and resentful.

By contrast, evening showers were much preferable. No one was waiting and we could linger unhurriedly. Even better, in the dry season the water would be lukewarm from the day's heat. We sang loudly when the shower was warm, imitating

Guyana Farewell   local pop singers or the recording stars of stage and screen.

Of course, a particularly strident effort or wayward note brought jeers and ridicule from anyone in earshot.

Our morning ritual as a family, which was compressed and complicated no matter what, was further affected by the rainy seasons. We had to leave the house in relays, our departures keyed by any momentary thinning of the downpour, and WE BLASTED OUT OF THE BOTTOM HOUSE, THROUGH THE GATE AND OVER THE BRIDGE, FEET PUMPING VIGOROUSLY AT OUR BICYCLE PEDALS, intent on getting as far as possible before taking shelter from the next downpour under the awning of a cake shop or grocery. It was not unusual to be marooned there for hours!

Sometimes we found our father, who normally left earlier, awaiting a break in the rain beneath the house. I remember the uneasy surprise I felt on seeing him abandon his usually controlled manner, pushing off from the house vigorously, pedaling furiously as he raised his umbrella overhead. Bicycles and umbrellas caused accidents. Riding during a temporary break in *Rains Came* the rain with one's umbrella hanging from your handlebars, a quick catch of the umbrella tip in the spokes and you'd have bruises and sodden belongings.

The rain might come down torrentially for as long as two days until the concrete drains between the picket fences and the grass borders of the streets overflowed with rushing torrents of water. During the rare but occasional pauses in the downpour, we crouched at the side of these drains and raced twigs and match sticks from wooden bridge to wooden bridge. Excitedly, we watched our "ships" bobbing and weaving on the surging rush of water, running alongside, urging our racer on and jeering at the efforts of friends. A misstep on the narrow grass border could plant a foot or shoe ankle-deep in the torrent, unless we'd had the time and foresight to remove our shoes first.

Sometimes we ventured into the alleyways that separated the backyards of houses on the parallel streets. Here the drains were larger and deeper.

They ran from street to intersecting street without the benefit of the little wooden footbridges at the

Guyana Farewell streetfront that permitted us to walk or ride our bikes from under the houses out onto the street. Here, races could be longer, because the verges on either side were wide enough to permit careful running, and the likelihood of being seen was less. We were generally forbidden to engage in any activity where we could not be easily observed or where we were likely to get our clothes damaged. There was the thrill of danger in the challenge of making the jump across the drain without falling in and getting soaked, and a lovely sense of solitariness the alleyways afforded. Also, if the rain resumed, as it often would without warning, and heavily, there was no readily available shelter – there was little access to the backyards of the houses and, often, the threat of watchdogs that would bark and bite.

We ran and slipped and slithered behind our racers, stifling our cries and laughter, suspended between the excitement of our competition and the anxiety caused by the imminent rain, ready at a moment's notice to abandon our pursuits at the sound of an inquiring voice or the first splash of a large raindrop.

We lived in a small, three-bedroom frame house similar to many others. It was made of wood like most of the houses in Guyana. Wood

Rains Came

was cheap and plentiful. A gallery ran the width of the house looking onto the street. Windows and shutters alternated along its length. The windows, glass-paned and opening outward, resembled French doors but stopped at waist height. The shutters hung from hinges on the top of the frame. They were pushed outwards and upwards by window sticks propped in holes at the bottom. At the ends of the gallery were bow windows. THE HEAT OF THE DRY SEASON CAUSED THE WOOD IN ROOFS AND WINDOWS TO SHRIVEL AND SHRINK. Our gabled wooden roof was covered with corrugated zinc sheets. At all the eaves, the corrugations of the zinc-sheeted roof emptied into U-shaped gutters that in turn drained into run-off pipes. In the rainy season, torrents of water cascaded off the roof into the drains, flowed through the run-off pipes and splashed noisily into the open drains outside the picket fences.

Guyana Farewell

During the early days of the rains, before we could identify and repair the damage, our house leaked constantly. Some days, it seemed as if every pot or pan was strategically placed throughout the house to catch water. Our excited shouts summoning an adult to the source of a new leak were a part of the hubbub. It was not uncommon to be awakened from the deep sleep of childhood to find the sheet wet from a surprise leak or even to be shocked awake by a splatter of water on top of the bed. Eventually, the leaks were identified and plugged or, AS THE WOOD OF OUR HOUSE SWELLED WITH MOISTURE, THE LEAKS DISAPPEARED.

Sometimes the roof gutters were clogged with debris – leaves, lost cricket balls, dead mice that had accumulated during the dry season. If left uncleared before the rains started, the debris created a damming effect. When the pressure of water finally shifted the blockage, unlucky passersby might find themselves inundated by a sudden deluge of water – to the delight of any children fortunate enough to witness their discomfiture.

More exasperating than the leaks, floods, muddy yards and damp *Rains Came* clothes were the constraints the rainy season placed on three or four energetic children in a small house on a Saturday. Once we had exhausted our surreptitious perusal of forbidden comic books and tired of board games, we inevitably devised some activity which brought warning shouts, threats and, eventually, swift physical chastisement. One day, we might play soccer with a bundle of newspaper rolled into a ball and secured with string, kicking and jostling and pushing in sheer animal pleasure. Other days, we'd climb into the rafters with towels tied as capes to imitate Superman or Batman, and jump down onto our beds with an accompanying shout at an imagined foe. Neither the iron frames nor the mattresses could long withstand such punishment and so became bent and battered.

Rain wrecked sports schedules and ruined wedding and funeral arrangements. It frustrated adult schedules for work and socializing. Rain-swollen creeks and rivers flooded roads and yards, drowned livestock and damaged goods incautiously stored at ground level. The lightning and thunder

that accompanied the onset of the season terrified us as small children. I remember huddling close to a nanny or caretaker, WHO TOLD US STORIES OF SPIRIT-LIKE JUMBIES AND TERRIBLE BAKOOS AND OF OLD HIGES THAT COULD CARRY US AWAY. The lightning was so intense that it flared and washed through our closed eyes and closed shutters, and the thunder crashed like enormous barrels hurled into empty caverns.

Older children relished the often interrupted school schedule. On days of the most torrential downpour, it was impossible to get to school without being completely soaked. We sheltered in groups for hours in shops and stores, confident that many of our teachers were similarly marooned. Those hardy enough to make it to school found themselves combined with students in other classes for casual sessions of conversation and leisurely reading – sessions that were wonderfully different from the usual strict and rigorous regimen. Outside the rain drummed and splattered against roof and windows, creating a cool, gray cocoon that engulfed and encapsulated us.

Most of the houses in our neighborhood had an exterior flight of stairs that ran parallel to the front of the house. At the top of the stairs was a small roofed platform, open on three sides, with a wooden railing not quite waist high, and balustraded, enabling a teenager or adult to hitch the edge of their backside comfortably as they chatted with friends, awaited company or hailed passersby. A young child could peer through the balustrades at the comings and goings of the street, see and announce oncoming family or friends a block or more away.

It is Saturday afternoon in Georgetown. The long morning of chores and errands is over. My brothers and I have consumed a substantial lunch of pigeon peas and rice, beef stew and fried plantains accompanied by a pitcher of freshly made limeade. Finally, free to entertain ourselves, we sit on the front steps of our house or lean on the little wooden gate that opens into our yard waiting for the arrival of our friends. As they drift in from similar preoccupations, we animatedly discuss, argue and plan the afternoon's activities. We are a grubby assortment of small boys in short pants and short-sleeved shirts, mostly barefooted. TROPICAL SUN BLISTERS THE ROWS OF SMALL ONE AND TWO-STORY HOUSES AND THEIR WHITE PICKET FENCES. Through the open windows, familiar sounds drift outward to us: sewing machines chatter, radios blare, shrieks of laughter and shouts of altercation alternate. Oblivious, we choose sides and identities for a game of cricket.

The city street, the somewhat tattered urchin preparing to launch a black, homemade balata ball down a gravel driveway disappear as the first batsman walks down the steps, through the gate of the picket fence and makes his way to the crease. Adjusting his imaginary protective gloves, he acknowledges the cheers of his teammates perched on the steps of the house. At the crease in front of

the wicket, he settles himself and then, for one majestic moment, steps back to survey the placement of the opposing fielders, to contemplate the distant boundaries of the playing field, and to scan the tumultuous crowd. He prepares to face the first bowler. Once more he settles himself and watches alertly as the bowler begins his long run and delivers the first ball. The ball bounces high and away. He lifts his bat disdainfully, allowing it to go by and into the gloves of the wicket keeper. His teammates shout appropriately admiring words that acknowledge his impeccable style and *sang-froid*.

All afternoon long the match continues as batsmen come and go and teams exchange places. Battered bats crafted from the branches of coconut palms, lopsided balls, bumpy fields and garbage-can wickets are transformed into the exquisite paraphernalia of professional teams. Clumsy amateur efforts become feats of polished execution, boasted about for days afterward.

If there was an important cricket series taking place locally or overseas, on the preceding or following days we often devised *My Town* special flourishes that enhanced our proceedings. A pitcher of ice water with a few tin cups might be ceremoniously delivered by a younger child, perhaps my brother Maxey, to the players – an imitation of the water breaks in the professional game during which two attendants in spotless white garb carried trays of cool drinks out to the field at intervals.

What times those were! Our imaginations ran rampant. There were international reputations to be made or ruined, endless opportunities to bat brilliantly, bowl effortlessly, perform with flair, conduct oneself with equanimity!

Happenings We lived on Robb Street in Georgetown, the capital city of Guyana. I recall sitting on the stairs that ran up the outside of our house and peering through the railings, fascinated by the women working in the street. EACH WOMAN WOULD SIT ON A SMALL WOODEN STOOL IN FRONT OF A PILE OF LARGE ROCKS. Using a heavy mallet, she would systematically reduce the rocks to pebble-sized pieces. The women wore wide-brimmed straw hats and the sweat would run down their

dark faces as they thumped and sorted all day long in the relentless sun. Each day they brought small, stacked aluminum containers, and at noon they would hungrily eat foo-foo and salt fish, or eddoes and cassava and smoked herring.

I didn't know then that these women were the vanguard of an army of workers that would eventually transform the gravel road we lived on to a smoothly paved asphalt street. After the women came, a crew of men arrived with their shovels and picks, ragged clothes, and an assortment of exotic headgear. Next came the wheelbarrows and spades of the spreaders, who distributed pebbles evenly on the bed of the street. Lorries delivered loads of sand in a manner which delighted us: THE WHOLE BED OF THE VEHICLE WOULD RISE AND TILT WITH A HIGH WHINING SOUND, until all the load began sliding and, gathering momentum, rushed out with a satisfying roar, making a wonderful pyramid at the roadside. If the lorries came late enough in the day, the sand would be there overnight, which gave us a

chance to compete at running to the top of the
sand pyramids, trying to get as high as possible

before sliding back or getting
stuck. The shrieks and laughter would inevitably draw
first the notice, then repri-
mands and, finally, if we were

uncooperative, swift physical retribution from
our parents.

At some point later in the paving process came
the heavy stone rollers with their operators, perched
imperiously in the small shelter atop the vehicle.
The rollers slowly crunched and ground the sand,
rocks and pebbles into a semblance of evenness in
preparation for the tar-making machines. These
machines were a source of enormous fascination to
us, with their pungent smell of boiling pitch,
their beds of glowing coals beneath the blackened,
ancient-looking boilers, and the buckets beneath
their spouts. We would edge closer to watch as
the workers filled the buckets with black, boiling
tar and, with admirable insouciance, poured it for
the spreaders to distribute smoothly.

Eventually, smaller rollers would arrive to put

a finishing touch on the job. At last the street lay in pristine gleaming perfection, though reeking for

days afterward. The new street was strangely smooth for bare feet to test tentatively, and for bicycles to move about in skidless certainty after years of gravel precariousness.

The Map of Home Robb Street, Oronoque Street, Albert Street, Regent Street, North Road: I never knew or cared about the origins of those street names. All I knew was that these streets constituted the boundaries of my earliest years. Beyond the white picket fences that surrounded the houses were concrete drains, a foot deep and equally wide. Grass borders extended in uniform width to where the surface of the street began. Except for the main thoroughfares where the buses ran, all the streets in the town followed this pattern. There were no sidewalks. WE WALKED ON THE ROAD PAST THE WHITE-PAINTED, RED-ROOFED WOODEN HOUSES, PICKET FENCES, CONCRETE DRAINS AND GRASS BORDERS. The houses had shingled roofs, and though some were two or three stories like my grandparents' house, most were one-story like ours, elevated on wooden or concrete posts to a height of ten feet or more above the ground. This architectural design was most practical. In the *My Town* rainy season, it prevented flooding and allowed ventilation. In the dry season, it permitted access to the sea breezes, those northeast trade winds that in the mornings and the evenings tempered the heat and brought cooling relief.

The wide main streets, with their bustle of stinking buses, donkey carts, bicycles, and busy sidewalks, provided a stark contrast to the quiet, almost somnolent atmosphere of our street. Camp Street was a boulevard – a tree-lined walkway flanked by one-way streets and bordered by large houses. Brickdam, with its large, densely-foliaged trees and mansions set back among gardens, had a tranquil feeling but its wide vistas hinted of pomp and ceremony and long-departed parades. Canals that flowed quietly down the middle of Church Street and South Road and bordered Lamaha Street and Vlissengen Road offered further variety to the pattern of our small colonial city.

Open Air Markets

Two open-air markets – Bourda and Stabroek – were the center of frenzied activity every morning except Sunday.

Bourda   Bourda market was near our home, opposite an open expanse of grass bordered by large trees known as Bourda Green. From the early hours of the day, vendors wended their way to the market in the darkness with huge baskets of fruit or vegetables balanced on their heads or riding in carts harnessed to donkeys. The carts had flat wooden beds suspended on large, spoked wooden wheels with metal or rubber rims that grated or hummed on the gravel roads leading into town. These donkey cart men, as they were known, were required to have a lighted lantern at the rear of their carts after dark so that bicyclists or motor vehicles would avoid colliding with them.

Long before dawn each morning, the donkey carts with lanterns suspended below the cart beds and swinging with the motion of the carts, filled the coast road as they made their way from villages with names like Mahaica and Buxton, Plaisance and Cane Grove, Belfield and Enmore. IN THE DARKNESS, RELIEVED ONLY BY THE GLIMMER OF STARS, THE LANTERNS DIPPED AND SWAYED LIKE SO MANY FIREFLIES. Sleeping drivers depended on their plodding donkeys to make their way into town along the city streets to the markets. The donkey cart men were a ragged, illiterate, independent breed. They contracted to deliver goods and, occasionally, passengers. They often scandalized Guyana's sober citizens with their profanities, loud altercations and sporadic fights.

"Clear the way for I'm a-coming," they would chant,
"Comin in a jackass cart.
De shaft got rotten and de wheel got broken,
And the jackass began to p h a r t."

My uncle Ivan recalls that as a mischievous
teenager, he and his friends quietly and carefully

Guyana Farewell   reversed the direction of one of
the donkey carts in the early
morning, sending the cart and
its contents back home as the unwitting driver
snored loudly. The imagined spectacle of the bewil-
dered and irate driver waking to find himself
and his load on his own doorstep in the morning
sunshine provided Uncle Ivan and his delinquent
friends with great hilarity for many years after.

On market days, gaily painted wooden buses,
jammed with market women and loaded with produce in the rooftop bins, would also be using the
coast road. Sporting names that ran the gamut
from sober to bizarre, from strait-laced to comic –
Just In Time, No Time To Die, Rock-a-Bye Baby,
Decision Before Dawn, Berbice Express – the rickety buses careened through the night. In the darkness before dawn, they would occasionally slam
into an unlit donkey cart or one that failed to pull
into the curb quickly enough. Enormous altercations ensued as passengers, bus driver, donkey cart
men and passersby traded insults, invective and

profanities at the tops of their voices.

"Oh Gawd! Yuh kill meh chickens!"

"Mahn, yuh drivin' lak *Open Air Markets* *yuh crazy! Wha' happen to yuh lights, yuh son of a jackass!"*

All the while their livestock cackled and bleated, and the donkeys brayed loudly. Finally, a constable from the nearest village would arrive on his bicycle to arbitrate.

Bourda market filled a complete city block bounded by streets and sidewalks. Rows of wooden stalls were roughly divided into areas according to different types of commodities: fish, meat and poultry, fruit and vegetables, herbs and spices, grains and cereals, school supplies, sewing supplies and dress patterns, slippers and shoes, secondhand books and sundries of all sorts. STALLS WERE PRESIDED OVER BY A MOTLEY ASSORTMENT OF VENDORS. Most of them had maintained their stalls for years and were known by name to their customers, mostly housewives and maids shopping for their daily meals. Most homes, including ours in my early childhood years, had no refrigerators. This necessitated daily shopping for all but the staples such as rice, plantains, dried peas and beans.

"Well, look at you, dear, in yuh fancy new hat!

*Yuh mus' be meetin' yuh
boyfren'."*

*"Freddie, yuh bettah keep yuh
mout' off a me! Yuh gettin' too fresh."*

All morning long the vast expanse of the market would resound with loud bargaining, profane bantering, and colorful greetings. Many an argument arose, punctuated by indignant accusations of short weight or price gouging.

*"Tek yuh finga' off de scale, yuh ole scampion!
Yuh tink ah don' see yuh!"*

*"Put in a extra one fah me, mahn! I is a good
customah!"*

Rising above the cacophony of voices in a soaring fretwork of intricate iron struts and supports was a painted cast iron roof with steeples and buttresses and ornamentation characteristic of Victorian construction. Open on the sides with an outer, unsheltered section, these markets would be permeated, in the rainy season, with the rattle of rain on the roof, a deep, murmurous roar of voices, the pungent aroma of assorted scents and smells –

all superimposed on a background of bright garments, elaborate multicolored headdresses and an array of seasonal merchandise *Open Air Markets* hanging from the roofs of the stalls. There were kites at Easter, toys and dolls at Christmas and sporting goods at other times. In the outdoor stalls, large black umbrellas sheltered the vendors, AND THE COLORFUL HEAPS OF FRUIT AND VEGETABLES WOULD GLEAM WET IN THE RAIN. The scent of overripe fruit filled the air, while brilliant splashes of yellow and orange, green and purple offered a treat to the eyes.

Converging on the markets was the traffic from the small wooden train that ran on a narrow gauge track along the coast between two major rivers, the Demerara and the Berbice. Belching black smoke from its engine, the train arrived in the early morning, delivering scores of passengers laden with baskets of produce and a motley assortment of livestock. They descended on the donkey carts, local buses and pushcarts with a clamor of demands for service, transport or assistance.

"Pick up dem bags fuh me, mahn. Bring dem ovah to de Eas' Bank bus."

"Wheah yuh goin', missee? I can tek yuh deh fas-fas!"

Guyana Farewell

"Look out deh! Ah comin' tru!"

Depending on the season, the scene would be one of morning darkness, giving way to rays of the early sun. First light revealed colorfully dressed market women, mostly black but also brown-skinned East Indians, involved in animated exchanges with tattered and bedraggled donkey cart men, pushcart drivers or the more soberly clad bus drivers, for transport to the markets. Many trying to get to the market would be barefoot, others wearing cheap rubber sandals. When it rained, the huge black umbrellas mushroomed everywhere and, in the downpour, EVERYONE CLUSTERED UNDER AWNINGS OR DRAPED THEMSELVES IN TATTERS OR TARPAULIN, wore cardboard boxes or sweltered in heavy, black rubber raincoats as they busily argued, negotiated and bargained their way to the markets.

Stabroek Market From across the Demerara river, the ferry would bring equally heavy traffic from the west coast. Vreed-en-hoep, the ferry terminal and village opposite Georgetown on the river, was a small characterless community that seemed to exist solely as a transfer point for traffic. For passengers awaiting the *Open Air Markets* ferry in the cavernous wooden building open on the sides, the wide brown river could be end- lessly fascinating. Darkened

with silt from its many tributaries, sluggish and turgid in the dry season, rushing and relentless in the rain, it pulled and tugged at the huge pilings that supported the wharf, sucking and thumping and gurgling beneath our feet, creating a feeling of impermanence and instability when it caused the structure to tremble and shudder.

As the faint glow from a lightening sky allevi- ated the darkness, the bustle of porters, the thump of heavy sacks, the rolling of drums and barrels, the conversations of passengers and vendors going to Stabroek market, all seemed strangely muted and expectant until the ferry appeared in the distance. Then the sounds would rise to a crescendo.

"Doris! Doh-riis!! Wheah yuh deh? Bring dem bags quick! Leh we get a good place."

"Watch out! Watch out! Ah comin' tru!"

"Oh, Ras, mahn! Wha' yuh doin? Gimme a han', nuh!"

Guyana Farewell

When the ferry reversed into the berth, handlers secured it with thick ropes to enormous pilings made of greenheart logs, famous worldwide for their toughness and resistance to water. Heavy wooden ramparts were lowered with a resounding thud that echoed through the terminal. These would be barely secured before everyone would rush aboard in an undisciplined, jostling mass trying to establish a space for their bags and baskets, hampers and bundles. Many of these passengers would already be engaged in commerce long before the ferry reached the Stabroek market dock on the other bank.

Stabroek, the larger of the two markets, was a sprawling establishment on the bank of the river. Its tower and clock were well-known landmarks at one end of Water Street. Because it adjoined the long row of docks where river steamers and ocean-going vessels berthed, it catered to a larger constituency than the smaller, more local Bourda market. Stabroek's stalls and booths were larger and better lit. Its aisles and passages were wider and more accessible. A fair portion of its transactions were wholesale to local merchants *Open Air Markets* supplying their dry goods stores and small groceries.

FISHING BOATS DELIVERED THEIR CATCH TO THE MARKET'S WHARVES DAILY FOR SALE on consignment to the market's fish stalls or to the owners of fish markets elsewhere in Georgetown.

The different sections of Stabroek were easily distinguishable. One large area was devoted to the low, tray-like stalls of the fruit and vegetable vendors. These vendors were exclusively women, many of them well-known characters whose smiling banter and loud, extravagant welcoming of their customers went far to conceal the shrewd, knowledgeable bargaining that ensured their survival.

"Look a' dese lovely mangoes, madam. Yuh can't get bettah nowheah!" they cried.

"Doan bother with she! Come, sweetheart. Ah give you a good bargain."

They presided over stalls bursting with seasonal fruits and vegetables: ripe yellow and red mangoes, pale brown sapodillas, purple luminescent star-apples, fat green soursops and tiny genips, pale, yellow sun-ripened limes, bright yellow fivefingers

and cimatoos, dark red sorrel and jamoons, Surinam cherries and seaside grapes, oranges and yellow papaws. Heaps of fresh peppers – tiny red and green 'wiri-wirris' and long, tapered yellow and green bird peppers – rested beside yams and sweet potatoes, cassavas and eddoes, breadfruit and plantains.

SUFFUSED IN A BOUQUET OF SCENT, THE VENDORS CALLED AND CAJOLED, TEASED AND TEMPTED as they worked against the day's deadlines and the impermanence of their produce.

"Look heah, darlin'. Try dese sapodillas. Dey ripe fuh eatin'! Yuh goan like 'em."

In another area that reeked of fresh meat and blood, the stalls were owned by butchers who hacked and sliced at haunches of beef, mutton and pork in response to the demands of housewives and maids. The stalls these vendors worked in were large wooden affairs with their owners' names formally lettered at the top, front and sides. Carcasses hung from huge hooks on the ceilings and frames.

Further on was the fish market where, on

wide, low stalls for easier viewing, the catch of
the day gleamed black and silver, blue and red, pale
yellow and gray. Red snapper *Open Air Markets*
and bonito, grouper and yel-
low fin resting on ice beside
huge heaps of shrimp could be pointed out by
customers, examined, transferred to large old-fash-
ioned scales lined with brown paper or newspaper,
and purchased by the pound or whole. Freshwater
fish such as hassa, patwah, houri and cuirass was in
great demand and the relative merits would be discussed and argued with gusto by the vendors, the
male sellers adding salacious touches to the banter
with their mostly female customers.

"It so sweet, darlin'," as three or four hassa
would be handed over, *"jus' like you."*

Such sallies might be received with appreciative laughter or contemptuously disdained with a
rude sound made by pressing lips against teeth and
emitting air. This habit, called "sucking your teeth,"
was considered rude and uncouth. Woe betide the
child who was caught making such a sound to an
adult, usually behind his or her back.

Large barrels of dried mackerel, smoked her-

ring, and codfish could be found nearby in an area
that also offered sugar and spices, cereals and dried

Guyana Farewell   fruit, black-eyed peas, red beans
and yellow split peas. These
were displayed in huge burlap
bags, their tops peeled back to expose the produce
where small shovels were plunged, ready for use.
On the shiny brass scales, the vendors would heap,
stack or assemble appropriate piles of dried fish,
dried peas or brown or yellow sugar on pieces of
brown or gray wrapping paper, swiftly pouring,
measuring and wrapping, then tossing the shovel
deftly back into the storage bags or bins.

THE AIR IN THE DIM CAVERNOUS EXPANSE WAS
DUSTY AND FILLED WITH A POTPOURRI OF SCENTS.
Long shafts of light slanted downwards from huge
skylights in the arching metalwork of the roof.
There was a continuous drone – voices cajoling,
insulting, requesting; meat cleavers thudding; barrels grating and rolling; feet shuffling and slippers
slip-slapping. Sudden altercations would break out
here and there. Above the piercing whistles that
warned of the ferry's departure, the crazed braying
of jackasses from the holding area past the entrance
often seemed to continue interminably.

Sister Jones

Sister Jones, who was a fixture at Bourda market, is inextricably linked to the network of my childhood. I cannot recall exactly when she became a part of our lives – nor did I ever know her background. What is certain is that this market woman with her dark-brown lined face, her hoarse, kindly voice, her eyes that crinkled pleasantly at the corners when she smiled, became a constant in the life of our family. Her stall was favorably located on one of the central aisles that led into the market. There she always sat, her ready smile radiating a welcome any time one of us stopped by during the day to or from school or work. She would tender a fruit, reach into her capacious apron pockets or lift the edge of the paper lining of her stall to produce a coin – perhaps a penny or a sixpence, even a shilling. She held one of our hands or encircled a waist with her arm in those long ago days when we were still small enough to welcome affection, still without the inhibitions and reticence that adolescence eventually brought.

Sister Jones, unmarried and childless as far as I knew, was pulled into the orbit of our family by my mother, as were so many other people. YET UNLIKE MOST OF THOSE, WHO DRIFTED IN AND OUT OF OUR LIVES, SISTER JONES REMAINED to assume an important place and status, formalized when she moved into the cottage in the backyard of our house. I am not sure how my mother and Sister Jones became friends. It is a reasonable surmise that my mother's daily visits to Bourda market to purchase guavas during the season brought her into contact with Sister Jones. Most likely, Sister Jones' reliability in providing a dependable supply of the fruit yielded my mother's respect and thus began the friendship.

Because my mother deemed her primary mission in life as saving sinners from eternal hell and damnation, she always carried a supply of biblical

tracts that coupled verses from the Old and New
Testaments with exhortations to repent one's sins

Guyana Farewell and be saved. She never hesitat-
ed to engage anyone she
encountered as part of her com-
mercial activities, whether market vendor or merchant, entrepreneur or bureaucrat, in earnest discussion of their need to repent their sins and be
saved. How wonderful it is, she would urge them,
"to be washed in the blood of the Lamb," and to be
"in the service of the Lord." To see the slightly
stunned expression of some soberly attired civil servant facing my mother's earnest proselytizing was to
be entranced as a child, embarrassed as an adolescent and, much later, amused in the recollection.
MY MOTHER'S ENTHUSIASM AND PASSION WERE
OVERWHELMING; the hapless victim would wander
away clutching three or four Bible tracts, mumbling assurances of repentance and promises to
attend the revival meetings.

Whatever the circumstances of their initial
acquaintance, Mother and Sister Jones developed a
life-long relationship. On Sister Jones' part, it was a
compendium of respect, admiration, gratitude and

affection. It is more difficult to determine what my mother's perspective on the friendship was.

Her personal feelings were usually hidden behind a barrier of reserve, but there was, undeniably, respect and admiration for Sister Jones'

Sister Jones

independence, strength and kindness. What real affection there was can only be deduced from the fact that Sister Jones was eventually installed in the cottage in our backyard. She became a member of Mother's church and assumed the unofficial role of family friend, counselor, arbitrator of family disputes, confidante and consoler. My father's attitude toward Sister Jones was initially indulgent toward one of such lowly status, followed by growing respect and admiration, and finally became a mixture of affection and friendship.

How it came about that this market woman with her limited education, lowly social origins and lack of sophistication assumed such an important role in our family is as much a testimony to my mother's disdain for convention as to the force of her personality. Her regular patronage of Sister

Jones' stall indicated that she trusted her and depended on her, assuring Sister Jones' standing in the mar-

ketplace. More and more, Sister
Jones assumed the role of agent
in procuring and bargaining
for the produce my mother needed for her growing
cottage industry of jams, jellies and pastries. Perhaps
most important was Sister Jones' reliability and
unflappable demeanor in the face of my mother's
demanding regimen and overpowering personality.

Once the friendship began between them,
it was a friendship not so much of equals, but of
sponsor and beneficiary, of honorary older relative
and younger, vigorous, determined child. As did
so many who came into my mother's orbit, Sister
Jones regarded my mother with a mixture of affection, perplexity and awe for her single-mindedness,
her disregard for convention and her ability to
overcome obstacles. Sister Jones developed an
older sister's amused tolerance as she was pushed,
tugged, manipulated and bullied into first my
mother's employment, then her church and, finally,
her family.

For weeks before Easter, the stores and small shops were fully stocked with a colorful display of kites. Our small faces peered into shop windows and open doorways, intently examining the combinations of colors, the array of designs. Our young voices speculated knowledgeably on the relative merits of various sizes, different shapes, accoutrements and paraphernalia. We were able to watch the construction of kites in some shops. The frame was carefully assembled from pre-cut pieces of the lightest wood available. The predominant design was a six-sided shape, created by forming a star-shaped framework from three pieces of wood nailed at the center. Through holes at the ends of each piece, string was used to connect and establish the basic structure. Brightly colored, shiny kite paper was glued to the frame, forming multicolored patterns that delighted every eye and suited any taste. Kites came in various sizes – from six inches to veritable giants taller than six feet. Beside the standard hexagonal configuration, THERE WERE BIRD SHAPES AND BOX SHAPES, FISHES AND STARS and other shapes as varied as the imagination and ingenuity could contrive to get airborne.

Weeks of speculation and innumerable discussions with my brothers and friends preceded our careful assessment of available funds versus the range of size and price offered. Occasionally, the opinion of a respected adult or older sibling might be solicited. The day of decision finally came for me, and proud, beaming, I walked home with a kite carefully but casually hanging over the back of one shoulder, one hand securely grasping the loop to which, eventually, a ball of string would be attached. In the other hand would be a length of light rope, intended for use as a tail for the bottom of the kite.

Kite tails and loops, bulls and frills – we

absorbed the compendium of kite flying knowledge
with such utter concentration that any teacher would

Guyana Farewell have offered happily any number
of kites to get the same results
on their more mundane topics.

My new kite became the focus of my life.
I foraged among the pieces of colored cloth that
littered the floors of seamstresses and their sewing
machines. I WHEEDLED AND BARGAINED FOR A
BRIGHT SUPPLY. Then, carefully threading my collection into the length of rope for the kite's tail,
I worked to achieve the most brilliant display and
array of colors.

When all was complete, I could hang my kite
carefully and prominently from a rafter, a door or a
wardrobe, so that the first thing I saw on awakening in the morning was its splendor.

Hot Cross Buns The morning of Easter
Monday, a holiday in Guyana, was the traditional
kite-flying day, but long before that day arrived
many other traditions had to be observed. The
week before Easter, our mouths began to water
with the anticipation of hot cross buns. In the bak-
eries and cake shops through the town, trays of fra-

grant sweetbreads and cakes gleamed in sticky anticipation of eager, plundering fingers.

> *"Hot cross buns! Hot cross buns!*
> *One a penny, two a penny,*
> *Hot cross buns!"*

Our childish voices sang eagerly, as we gluttonously contemplated the soft sinking of teeth in freshly made hot cross buns, their shiny patina bisected by white crosses of frosting, and surfaces bursting with currants and bits of candied fruit. As children, hot cross buns seemed the aristocracy of baked goods, their deliciousness enhanced by the specialness of Easter.

Easter was also special as one of the two times each year that we would get new clothes, Christmas being the other. To a child whose wardrobe consisted of a few shirts, three or four pairs of short pants, two pajamas, a few singlets and socks, any addition of new clothes was a wonderful occasion. All of our clothes were made by Mrs. Hunter who lived nearby and who, like all the adults in our lives, seemed a baffling combination of scolding irascibility or

smiling approbation. Sent for a measurement at
the seamstress, one could expect to be tugged and

Guyana Farewell prodded like an inert lump,
occasionally pricked by a pin,
but always buffeted or cosseted
in a confusing but nevertheless diverting session.
This ritual was a part of Easter, as inevitable and
irresistible as the season itself.

At last came the day to try on our new finery!
Under the severe scrutiny of mother, Mrs. Hunter
would help me into a shirt that was carefully ironed
to best effect. She would button it down the front
and then button the sleeves, which were usually
long. THE ODDITY OF WEARING LONG SLEEVES ON
OUR SHIRTS IN THE HEAT OF THE TROPICS WAS
ONLY ONE OF THE PUZZLING SARTORIAL CUSTOMS IN
GUYANA. It was probably attributable to our slavish
emulation of the British who, coming from the
wet, cold climate of their home, brought long
sleeve shirts, gray flannel trousers and other practices, appropriate in England, bizarre in the tropics.

With a few tugs and adjustments from the
seamstress, I would then stand to be critically
appraised. If all seemed satisfactory, I was assisted

in donning my new pants. This latter ritual provided some amusement for Mrs. Hunter as my brothers and I grew older and *Easter* began to exhibit a predictable reluctance to change in the presence of supervising females. At last, the new outfit would be carefully folded and wrapped, and borne homewards with great pride.

Finally, Good Friday came. It always seemed an interminable day! The holiest day of the year, it was observed with a minimum of activity. The streets were deserted, voices seemed muted, radios played hymns or doleful music. Visions of tombs and graveyards, of naked thieves flanking a crucified Christ and groups of hooded, grieving women plagued our childish consciousness. Even the brilliant sunshine never seemed to relieve the pall of sadness and despair that prevailed and, confined to the house as we were, we longed for the company and conversation of friends, wandered restlessly from room to room, slept fitfully and barely endured the long day's darkness.

The first opportunity to wear our new clothes was Easter Sunday. Arrayed in our new outfits

which, if we were fortunate, would incorporate a
pair of shiny new patent leather shoes that always

Guyana Farewell   squeaked and hurt, we set off
for the special Easter morning
church service. As was true
for every aspect of the holiday, the Easter church
service involved much preparation by the congregation. The church had to be scrubbed, paint
retouched, the furniture repaired, flower pots polished and made ready to receive the bouquets of
flowers. In addition, for the women, there would
be weeks of selecting fabrics, careful scrutiny of pattern books and style books, flying visits to ribbon
and thread displays at the stores, and innumerable
animated discussions followed by hours of sewing
machine effort. All that preparation yielded a splendid, colorful, stylish display of homemade fashions.

From every direction they bore down on our
little white church on Charlotte Street, women of
every conceivable color and complexion, from
intensely black through every shade of brown to
sapodilla gold to white. What a flotilla of fashion-
able frocks – silks and satins, taffeta and tulle, all
crowned with hats of every conceivable style and

fashion! A brilliant, dazzling display of color and glamour to be discussed and debated and recreated for days thereafter, with animation and enthusiasm, admiration and ridicule, laughter and enormous satisfaction.

Easter

Inside the church, quiet murmurs of acknowledgment stirred those already seated when some arbiter of fashion arrived in elegant, understated array, contrasting dramatically with the flamboyant plumes of some aspiring upstart. Barely repressed gasps and smiles prevailed when a misguided unfortunate bustled in, CLAD IN A CHAOS OF CLASHING COLORS AND SIMPERING SELF-SATISFACTION. Once the service started, however, except for an occasional surreptitious glance to check the set of a hat or to confirm the exact color of an outfit, all attention was addressed to the vigorous hymn singing and clapping, the murmured responses to the admonitions and exhortations of the preacher and to appreciative acknowledgment of the choir.

Afterwards, what a flurry of compliments and greetings there was, as everyone lingered outside the church in the bright, hot sunshine. Perspiration would bead the brows of the men in their heavy,

inappropriate, but nevertheless carefully tailored suits of wool and worsted, flannel and gabardine, with an occasional renegade sharkskin. We waited impatiently, fidgeting in our new clothes as the adults talked and laughed, whispered malicious asides and thoroughly enjoyed themselves.

Then it was home for a lavish Easter lunch. Platters of black-eyed peas and rice, fried plantains layered in yellow and golden brown, stewed beef in gravy spiced with pepper sauce, and all accompanied by mauby or ginger beer poured from large glass pitchers tinkling with ice cubes.

ALL THE SUNDAY AFTERNOONS OF MY YOUNG CHILDHOOD SEEMED TO LAST FOREVER, but particularly on Easter Sunday. Confined to the house, we read, did our homework, listened to the radio quietly if our mother was at church (as she invariably was for most of Sunday), but, worst of all, we were required to take a Sunday afternoon nap. I remember lying in bed in what seemed unnatural repose, surrounded by the murmurous sounds of the neighborhood, conscious of my mother and father, brothers and sisters dozing in adjacent beds, other rooms. Dogs barked, radios *Easter* played, and the sound of voices drifted in through the open windows while I tried to lie quietly to avoid awakening my brother David, who slept in the adjoining bed.

On Easter Sunday this routine of napping was particularly trying. The silhouette of my kite hanging on the door, its colorful frills moving faintly in the breeze from the open window was tantalizing. All the pent-up waiting and expectation of the previous weeks threatened to burst forth from me in an uncontrollable spasm of energy and enthusiasm. I was not likely to allow it, however. Great displays of noisy enthusiasm, loud laughter, and raised voices were not encouraged in the constrained, Victorian atmosphere of middle-class homes and especially not on Sundays.

Those somber, somnolent Sundays of childhood, hard church pews and intolerably long sermons, restraints of all sorts! On those days the spirit, restless and eventually rebellious, yearned for the freedom of the outdoors. Sundays became the symbol of all my childhood frustrations and the eventu-

Guyana Farewell   al catalyst, in my late adolescence, for my defiance of my mother. I would, sometimes furtively, sometimes defiantly, disappear after lunch to meet with friends subject to less restrictions. Of course, I was rarely comfortable, as guilt assailed me or the fearful expectation of my mother turning up to embarrass me loomed.

On Easter Monday we were up well before dawn, hurrying to take showers and get dressed. Morning tea would be consumed with gusto – hot cocoa or tea with milk, large slices of homemade bread toasted and slathered with an orange-colored, salted butter and eaten with hunks of English cheddar. Our kites, glorious in their multicolored radiance, had been carefully hung the evening before in prominent places to greet our awakening eyes. The long rope tails intertwined with bits of colored cloth were neatly coiled. The balls of tightly wound kite string passed through the center of the coils. We hung the kites over our shoulders and held the balls of string securely in front.

The street lights would still be on when
we descended the front steps and filed out into the
street. Our excitement was *Easter*
intensified by the unfamiliar
ambiance of the early morn-
ing dark and the need to speak quietly to avoid
waking the neighborhood. The fragrance of flowers
and shrubs was delicate in the still morning air,
before the breeze and sunshine could dispel it.

Sometimes, as we were halfway to the seashore,
trudging up Camp Street where large, luxuriant
trees flanked the center path, the street lights would
go out and, in the half-dark that preceded dawn, we
exchanged delighted glances and smiles. Additional
contingents of similarly equipped and equally excited children emerged from side streets and enlarged
the growing columns of quiet kite fliers heading
for the seashore and the long awaited launching of
the kites.

Dawn would have cleared the morning sky
by the time we reached the seashore. We hurried to
find a good spot on the brown expanse of the beach
with sufficient room to launch our kites and avoid
entangling them with others. The morning tide was

always a concern. Ideally, it would be an ebb tide, the waves receding, to leave a wide, dry expanse

Guyana Farewell

of sand that provided a spacious venue for the occasion. Soon the cries of seabirds and the murmur of the waves would be drowned out by the excited shouts and laughter of children, the streams of instructions from parents and all the happy hub-bub of raising, sustaining and monitoring the kites. Lifted by the morning breeze thousands of kites would rise to fill the air for miles along the shore.

Kites of every conceivable color, size and shape danced and swayed, rippled and tossed, painting the skies with a constantly changing collage of color and movement. I REMEMBER THE RUSTLING OF THE FRILLS, THE BUZZING OF THE BULLS, THE SINGING OF THE KITES, and the murmur of the sea beyond – a splendidly satisfying cacophony, impossible to forget. Exotic shapes – stars and boxes, hexagons and diamonds – some as tiny as handkerchiefs, others so huge that they required two or more men to control the powerful pitching and tugging. And, always, there was the threat of razor blades. Attached to the tails of some kites by delinquents, they could sever a kite string and set a kite adrift in the sky. I can see, even now, that Easter morning long ago, my friend Joe Hazle- *Easter* wood, running frantically and calling in the hope that someone might grasp the trailing string before his kite, rising on an updraft, became irretrievable, its size diminishing with distance, its memory as flimsy and fragile as its substance.

Perhaps most affecting for me was the lovely rippling movements of the tiny frills of paper glued to the upper edges of many kites. They trembled and quivered in the breeze. Below, the long kite tails undulated sinuously, their pieces of multicolored cloth bright in the morning sun.

Easter Monday was a most satisfying experience for a young child. Nothing ever equaled that excitement of rising early, making the long trek from darkness to dawn surrounded by the sense of gathering friends and strangers under the vista of sea and shore and sky. Then, the thrill of our kites rising, in jerks and starts, the wonderful sense of a community of children and parents free of its usual restraints, filled with a sense of all things possible.

School Days

Out into the quiet street the sing-song voices of the children carried as they chanted: *"One and one are two, two and two are four..."*

The two-story building at the corner of Camp and Middle Streets in a quiet residential area was one of many similar schools throughout the town and country. Christ Church Elementary School which I attended, from age six to twelve, was run by Mr. Walker, a stern principal, with a no-nonsense manner, much admired by parents.

A main stairway led from the schoolyard to the wide double doors of the upper floor, into a spacious room. This room was divided into sections, each reserved for a class. There were no partitions between the classes; it was, in effect, a one-room school. Grade levels were called standards, and each group of students was a class. Kindergarten and pre-kindergarten were referred to as ABC and Little ABC. At Christ Church Elementary, these classes were located on the lower floor with their own access. This bottom floor was raised about three feet off the ground to prevent flooding in the rainy season, and was partially walled by a wooden lattice work that allowed air to circulate. Part of the playground was sheltered by the jutting out of the second floor. This permitted students a sheltered outdoor space to mill around on during the rainy season, but it was not much of a sanctuary on days when rain poured and wind blew.

Because there were no partitions between the classes, there was a constant cacophony through which teachers taught and children absorbed the lessons. Since many sessions involved reading aloud, spelling aloud or chanting responses as a group, THE HUBBUB WAS CONSIDERABLE. I suppose that most children learned early on to tune out anything that was not of consequence to them. For children with learning disabilities, a term then

unknown and a condition probably unacknowledged, it must have been intolerable.

Guyana Farewell   In the earliest classes, we wrote
on slates with slate pencils.

Slates, framed in wood, came
in two sizes, and could be purchased at the small,
ubiquitous corner shops that carried general merchandise. TO DROP AND BREAK ONE'S SLATE WAS ONE
OF THE MANY SMALL TRAGEDIES THAT WERE A PART
OF CHILDHOOD. As we moved into higher classes,
we used copy books and small lined exercise books
and began writing with pencils and pens.

Spilling ink on a copybook from the inkwells
inset in the small wooden desks was another disas-
ter. The pens we used were standard. Made of
wood, available in differing colors, they tapered six
inches to a point from a small, round and flat base
with a curved slit into which the nibs were inserted.
Nibs made a difference. They came in a variety of
styles, permitting individuality in penmanship,
depending on how fine or broad the points were.
To be constrained to use nibs that we were unaccustomed to, was a dismaying prospect at any time.
To be thus equipped at examination time was a

serious problem. It impeded our speed, caused blots and generally agitated us into errors and tears.

Rote learning, memorization, slogans and corporal punishment were the order of

School Days

the day. We wrote interminably in our copy books, in carefully crafted cursive, such initially incomprehensible bromides as: "Don't carry coals to Newcastle;" "A stitch in time saves nine;" and "Penny wise, pound foolish." We memorized and regurgitated on cue such civilizing admonitions as: "Don't spit about, spitting is insanitary;" "Cover your mouth when you cough or yawn;" and, "Children must be seen and not heard." We sang, recited, responded and muscled our way through a traditional curriculum of reading, writing, spelling, handwriting, arithmetic, Anglican religious training, and, occasionally, some nature study and music, which meant singing.

Teachers received certificates from teacher training institutes that qualified them to teach in public schools. I remember these teachers, for the most part, as strict but caring, ready to smile, quick to forgive, exasperated by chatterboxes or dunces, while varying in their propensity to use a straight ruler to punish the tardy, the sluggard, or the irre-

pressible. They were consistent in their prompt chastisement of any child considered rude.

Rudeness in children was a cardinal sin in our small colonial Victorian society. A teacher would box our ears, expel us instantly from class, or even strike us a few times on our open palms with a ruler. Most of these responses were regarded as justified by adults, though occasionally someone might demur if the punishment seemed excessively harsh. We were rarely in doubt of what constituted rude behavior. It ranged from extremely subtle gestures, such as a certain type of facial expression called "cutting your eye" (as in "don't cut your eye at me") to something as overt as making a rude sound, most likely sucking one's teeth. "Don't suck your teeth at me!" was often heard.

Personal hygiene was emphasized. Teeth, nails and clothes were inspected regularly by teachers. Our hair had to be combed and neat. At some schools, girls were not allowed to wear their hair loose. It had to be braided or clipped back. Sheila, my sister, had long braids that extended down her back. I remember her standing glumly as my mother oiled and braided her hair tightly. As we returned from the playground each day, we carefully straightened our clothes and tucked in our shirts and blouses.

School Days

How fervently we sang at school assemblies! Indoctrinated from earliest childhood with the glories of the British empire, suffused with patriotism by innumerable renderings of the British national anthem, HOW ENTHUSIASTICALLY WE SANG FAMILIAR LYRICS ON EMPIRE DAY, the official birthday of the reigning British monarch.

> *The Empire too,*
> *We can depend on you,*
> *Freedom alone, these are the chains nothing*
> *can break.*

On Empire Day, we proudly paraded behind the police and militia bands. Marching in carefully dressed ranks in our school uniforms, serious as befitted such an important occasion, we made a smart "Eyes right!" as we moved quickly by

Government House. The British governor, attired in ceremonial dress and white topee, accepted our

Guyana Farewell

accolade from a raised podium. Standing at ease in the hot mid-morning sunshine on the parade grounds, we listened to patriotic addresses and stirring military marches played by the assembled bands. We cheered wildly, following a display of precision marching by the local militia and gazed with admiration as brilliantly uniformed police on horseback performed maneuvers, raising and lowering their lances at a trot and a gallop. Finally, the presentation of arms and a formal dismissal followed, allowing us to return to our schools or homes, talking and laughing as we regaled each other with the days's happenings.

Every day the iceman came. We could hear
the shrill blast of his whistle blocks away. The steel
girding the wooden wheels of his cart grated harsh-
ly against the pebbles in the street. The quiet,
gray donkey walking patiently between the shafts
seemed indifferent to the flutter of maids and their
derisive banter, the whistle blasts and the cool dripping of melting ice. Damp, brown burlap bags
were peeled back, exposing large, blocks of ice. The
ice man's small ax clove the air and split off with a
satisfying "thunk" the precise amount requested,
which clattered into the scales for formality's sake.
Then the purchase was thrust into a bag or a bucket
and borne away swiftly to a dark, cool place – for

lemonades, fresh fish, fruit salads, headaches, ginger beer and, on special days, ice cream!

Ice cream days! Cream and eggs and essence days. Ice cream days were two-whole-blocks-of-ice days, which immediately alerted every observant child to the imminence of the treat. THE EMPTY, STEEL-RIBBED, WOODEN CHURNS WAITING ON THE BACK STAIRS IN THE HOT AFTERNOON SUN are symbols of my childhood. How well I remember the cool, steel cylinders, half-filled with the rich cream and the heady scent of vanilla essence, being carefully centered in the churns, the breaking of ice into pieces that fit, the packing of ice and the coarse salt. "Don't forget the salt, Gladys," a relishing little voice would call. Then the churning, the taking of turns, the sweet sense of the tightening arm and, oh, the pervasive fragrance as pale, cool richness overflowed onto eagerly testing fingers.

At home, ice cream was the special treat reserved for birthdays and, to preside possessively over such a treat, served with cake, was a prideful pleasure that equaled opening one's gifts. Ice cream was preeminent in our hierarchy of sweets, but there were many more that we relished: toffee balls, bullseyes, never-done, ginger cake, rice cake, nutting, sour balls, lemon drops, brown, red and

Guyana Farewell

white sugar cakes, pearah and jilaybee, pink stretch candy, lollipops and peppermints, jube-jubes and butterscotch balls.

Sweets! How we loved them! How marvelous it was to sit on the front steps of our house sucking a never-done until one's jaws hurt, or to saunter aimlessly with a small friend, sharing a lollipop. Standing before the row of glass jars at the corner shop, clutching two or three pennies, we would endlessly debate the respective merits of color, flavor and quantity under the watchful, amused eye of the proprietor. From a spike that held pieces of plain, gray, inexpensive paper, the shopkeeper would detach an appropriate-sized piece. Carefully observed by the small customers, he would thrust a spoon into the jar of choice. THE LOVELY SOUND OF SWEETS RATTLING IN THE SPOON AGAINST THE GLASS MADE US SQUIRM IN HAPPY ANTICIPATION. Half a dozen sweets would be deposited in the small square of paper, then folded and twisted securely at the top and delivered into our waiting hands. We walked slowly away, intent on making the first selection, oblivious of the smiles of adults, totally engrossed in the antici- *Sweet Dreams* pation of the first blissful flood of sweetness as we sucked noisily. Despite the familiar anguish of toothaches in a society where dentists were a luxury, everyone – adults almost as much as children – indulged a taste for sweets. When I was quite young, locally made boiled sweets constituted the bulk of sweets available. The fragrance of boiling syrup or a glimpse of trays of vari-colored sweets freshly made at Dazill's, the local sweet shop, would start our juices running. Every adult was familiar with the endless childhood refrain: "Can I have a frek for a nutting? Please for a penny to buy sugarcake?"

In the sweet shops, the goods would be stored in endless rows of glass jars, usually by color – red, green, lemon, pink, rainbow – with the most popular choices in prominent positions. The shops were small, with a long wooden counter running the length of the space and two or three wooden doors that opened outwards from the middle, like French windows, onto the grass-bordered streets. These allowed easy access and also permitted passersby to quickly appraise the offerings.

Guyana Farewell   In addition to the rows of glass jars of sweets in these shops, there were, usually, one or two glass cases resting on the counter. These had small wooden doors that opened outward at the back so that the shopkeeper could reach in from behind the counter. They held selections of larger items such as coconut sugar cakes – some brown, others red and white – and ginger cakes or sticky concoctions that might attract flies. Although they were called cakes, this meant only that they were shaped like small cakes, but had neither the texture nor substance of cakes. Sugar was the basic ingredient, whether flavored with essences – vanilla, lemon, and orange – or mixed with grated coconut or crystallized ginger; it provided a cheap, easily obtained base for all the confectionery in Guyana.

Sugar, rice, timber and bauxite were the important export products of Guyana, but sugar and its many by-products – in particular, rum – dominated local commerce. Sugar plantations with their acres of tall sugar cane, green and yellow in the sunshine, filled the landscape, rivaled only by the rice paddies. During the harvest, the air, even in Georgetown, would often be filled with drifting ash from the fires set on the planta- tions. Besides the canals that bordered or bisected the

plantations, teams of mules plodded along well-worn tracks, pulling huge iron barges loaded with bundles of sugar cane. Men labored in the fields under the burning sun, their brown and black tor-sos gleaming with sweat, cutting the tall plants with cutlasses. Sugar refineries with their multiple smoke stacks belching steam and fire were every-where along the coast. DURING THE SEASON, FIRE FROM THE HUGE BOILERS GLOWED RED IN THE NIGHT. The smell of molasses filled the air.

Demerara sugar! The name was familiar throughout Britain and the Empire. Demerara was the name of the river and county where the capital, Georgetown, lay, and it gave its name to all sugar exported from Guyana. Needless to say, the planta-tions, the refineries, the ships and the sugar were all owned by British commercial interests. In Guyana,

the dominant name in commerce was Booker
Brothers. As Booker's went, so went the interests of

the colony, or so it seemed.

The sugar available to Guyanese
came in two basic forms: dark
crystal and yellow crystal. The local grocers stocked
both kinds in 100-lb burlap bags. They used metal
and wooden scoops to shovel it onto their curved
metal scales, selling it in one-lb or two-lb packages.
The kind of sugar crystal used in homes reflected
that household's taste and budget. Dark crystal
sugar was less refined and cheaper. The crystals,
particles of sugar, were coarser than those of the
pale, yellow crystal sugar, the popular choice for
limeade, tea tables and social functions. For important occasions such as weddings, birthday parties
and holiday celebrations, only imported white
sugar was considered for the elaborately iced cakes.

Packages of refined white sugar had to be purchased at the grocers. This commodity, imported
from Great Britain, represented the final stage of
Guyana sugar. It illustrated perfectly the economic
strategy that enabled a small group of islands to
draw enormous wealth and power from colonies

and territories worldwide. Produce raw materials in appropriate climates, do the initial refining locally, transfer in bulk using British *Sweet Dreams* ships, complete the manufacture and refining of product in home factories, package and ship out in British ships to markets in the colonies closed to other nations. Ownership of every stage of production, transport, manufacture and sale conferred enormous wealth, power and, of course, superiority.

Music Lessons

The sound of scales playing interminably on the piano or violin lingers forever in my vanished home. Music books piled on piano benches, violin bows were haphazardly deposited on tables. The calm voice of Mr. Bunbury, our music teacher for more than ten years, was endlessly suggesting, admonishing or approving. These images form a collage of childhood afternoons when the seemingly endless sessions droned on AS THE DUST MOTES DANCED IN THE RAYS OF SUNLIGHT STREAMING THROUGH THE WINDOWS. All of my siblings achieved some measure of skill with piano or violin; I was the one exception. My two older brothers, Patrick and Ronald, and my sister, Sheila, became quite accomplished. But only my younger brother David, persisted in his pursuit of music, working assiduously to become proficient in both classic and flamenco guitar.

Music examinations were created and administered by the Royal Society of Music. These tests, regularly scheduled, helped establish a student's level of proficiency in performance, music reading and notation. Lined music sheets inscribed with carefully rendered notes – clefs, stops, semi-quavers – were as much a part of our daily routine as the copy books we used in school. (Those unforgettable books, filled with meticulous, cursive handwritten slogans of relentless goodwill: "A stitch in time saves nine;" "A penny saved is a penny earned.") I preferred my own versions of these slogans which, though only mildly sacrilegious, inevitably yielded swift reprimand and swifter punishment.

My resistance to music lessons, like my resistance to so many rituals I experienced growing up in Guyana, stemmed less from a dislike of music than the tedious practice sessions. What irked me was the endless concentration on and repetition of the essentials: scales and notation in studying

music, conjugations and irregular verbs in
French and Latin; dates and place names in

Guyana Farewell   history and geography.
                                                   Heresy bubbled constantly in
                                                   my consciousness. Couldn't we
play some music by ear? Pick out simple tunes?
Work on pronunciation and simple conversation?
Discuss history in terms of actions and conse-
quences, geography in terms of human settlements
and endeavors? It seemed to me that everything
important was constantly obscured by the trivia of
dates and data, so much so that we seemed to
trudge through our days mired in the muddy ruts
of rote practice in subjects, never to reach the cut
and thrust of discussion, the exhilaration of performance, the inspiration of competition.

It amused me to learn years later that my
brother Patrick, the eldest child in the family, whom
I considered a paragon of virtue, hated his Saturday
afternoon lessons at Mr. Bunbury's house, yearning
to be away on sports fields with his friends.

Exactly when my parents concluded that it
was useless to continue my musical education is
hard to pinpoint. Perhaps my music teachers were

the first to characterize me as hopeless. It could be the futility of constantly chastising me dawned on my mother. Whatever the *Music Lessons* reason, the time came when I was released from the tedium of music lessons. But I never lost the yearning to be able to play the piano and, perhaps, if I had been encouraged to pick out tunes and if I had been helped with the finger placement, rather than inundated with technique and trivia, the time would have come when I wanted to learn the details.

MUSIC WAS AN IMPORTANT PART OF OUR LIVES IN GUYANA. It accompanied and enhanced most of our activities. Fortunately, music lessons constituted only a small part of this preoccupation, but represented the strong, traditional underpinning of all our singing and dancing, drumming and shaking, listening and whistling. We listened endlessly to all types of popular singers, admiring indiscriminately Sarah Vaughan and Patti Page, Enrico Caruso and Richard Tauber, Bing Crosby and Nat King Cole. We would stand transfixed at home or in the street, listening to radios as the matchless voice of Richard Tauber sang:

"I think that I shall never see
A poem lovely as a tree..."

Guyana Farewell   We laughed at local singers and
ridiculed pitilessly their efforts
to sound like the famous croon-
ers, despite our own feeble efforts to do the same.

Mr. Bunbury and Aunt Edna   Mr. Bunbury,
our violin teacher, came to our home sometimes,
while at other times we went to his studio for a lesson. But piano lessons were given by my godmoth-
er, Aunt Edna Jordan, at her home. And even
though only my sister Sheila, took piano lessons,
the memory of Aunt Edna lingers with me.

In many ways, Aunt Edna's home epitomized
the strong push for social standing through education and culture that characterized our small colonial society, a society steeped in the lessons of
Victorian Britain. In families like hers and my
grandparents', certain ideas were carefully inculcat-
ed from early childhood. DISCIPLINE WAS CRUCIAL.
Attending school and applying oneself assiduously
to learning ensured the academic standing that led
to a good civil service position. Coupled with
the appreciation of art and music through private

lessons and regular exercise on the sports fields, this regimen turned out a well-rounded person. The economic security of a civil *Music Lessons* servant's job, and the patient rise through the ranks per-mitted the acquisition of the symbols deemed important. The symbols were those of our British masters: neat, carefully fenced homes and gardens; small, well-maintained automobiles; sober, custom-tailored suits of British fabrics; flowered dresses and hats; good manners, moderation in everything and the observation of rules. It produced a careful, respectful citizenry in a well-ordered society. They also produced an occasional rebel.

Aunt Edna's home, a solidly built, two-storied house on Regent Street, was about two blocks away from ours. It exuded respectability with its neat, carefully painted exterior, and the small, yet well-tended flower garden behind the white picket fence. A small British motor car, always washed and gleaming, rested in the garage below the house, and I recall the luxurious scent of its dark, comfortable leather seats.

None of this affected my childish pleasure and

awe when, after being enveloped in the substantial perfumed embrace of Aunt Edna, I would sit,

waiting to be served a glass of mauby or sorrel with ice cubes coolly clinking. I had a chance to survey the dark, polished floors, the gleaming brass pots with their green plants, the heavy curved mahogany furniture, the grand piano, open and waiting, and the enormous floor model radio with its mysterious panels and array of shining knobs.

IT ALWAYS SEEMED COOL AND DIM AT AUNT EDNA'S, her curtains drawn to temper the hot, brilliant afternoon sunshine. Her wide smiling face would beam upon me as she offered sweet biscuits and asked the same questions she always asked. I would almost wriggle with pleasure to be the sole object of her attention.

I can't recall ever seeing Sheila having a piano lesson at Aunt Edna's. Nor can I imagine, either, that she would have her knuckles rapped as I occasionally did by Mr. Bunbury. A light-skinned man of medium height, eyes gleaming behind gold-rimmed glasses, I remember seeing him on his way to our house with his short, quick steps that seemed somehow effeminate. His occasional wry remarks at my expense, his slightly forced smile and unctuous manner when talking with

Music Lessons

my parents, always caused me to be somewhat uncomfortable in his presence and may have contributed to my lack of enthusiasm for music lessons.

Aunt Edna's pupils always took prizes at the music festivals. Was there a rivalry among the cadres of music teachers? Since the results of each category of competition were reported daily in the newspapers, replete with photographs, I don't doubt that the teachers maintained scrapbooks carefully detailing the accomplishments of their young prodigies. These results were probably more important economically to teachers such as Mr. Bunbury. He and others like him depended on maintaining a full schedule of music pupils for their livelihood, while Aunt Edna, with her small family, had a husband with a good civil service job.

The Music Festivals Music festivals were much anticipated and important events. Scheduled every two years, they were organized and administered by the Music Teacher's Association and were enthusiastically supported and participated in by schools,

Guyana Farewell   social clubs, civil service groups and churches. There were many categories of competition and levels of performance. During the fortnight of competition one could attend any of a variety of sessions, depending on one's interest.

For weeks prior to a festival, rehearsals of students, choirs, and ensembles were constant and intense. Private music teachers were an important element of our society and, during this period, they maintained a frantic schedule of practice sessions for their aspiring pupils. Piano and violin predominated in the festival performances. The sound of students running these instruments through their scales or rendering familiar classical melodies was a usual part of daily life, but during festival time rehearsals reached a veritable cascade of sound, spilling out of the open windows of schools and homes in every neighborhood.

Choral music achieved its highest recognition at music festivals. Of the many categories represented, my memory is most flooded with the sound of the men's choirs. My sister, on at least one occasion, trained and conducted a choir at a music festival.

I recall my intense pride as I beheld this small, elegantly coifed and dressed figure conducting and guiding with calm precision a large group  of singers. The choir produced a beautifully controlled and thrilling performance – music unfamiliar to me beforehand, but which I remembered long afterward.

The final event of each festival was the special concert given by the winners in each category. The recital hall would be packed with friends, relatives, music lovers, music teachers, officials and dignitaries. EVERYONE WAS DRESSED IN THEIR BEST OUTFITS. Men wore dark suits, white shirts and ties; women wore stylish hats, and dresses and gowns designed specially for the occasion; children were carefully brushed and neatly dressed, their shoes shining and manner subdued. Well before the concert was scheduled to begin, the hall would start to fill. A quiet hubbub of greetings, muted welcoming of friends, hugs and kisses for children, and a flutter of fans prevailed as anticipatory murmurs rose and fell. A hush would fall as the master of cere-

Guyana Farewell

monies appeared to welcome the audience. Finally, the concert would begin.

Throughout the performance the audience maintained rapt attention with occasional audible sighs of pleasure at some familiar piece of music. Sometimes a quiet ripple of amusement or special appreciation would tremble through the gathering at the rigidly erect posture of a young performer or the punctilious manner of some well-known musician.

Afterward, the audience would mill around inside and outside the hall offering congratulations to parents and performers, discussing a particular recital with much animation, reminiscing about prior festivals, and evincing a clear reluctance to end the excitement and pleasure of the occasion.

HOW DISTANT AND TRANQUIL IT ALL SEEMS NOW. The slow, quiet unfolding of seasons, the unhurried progression of nursery school, elementary school, high school, the cricket matches and holiday parades, church concerts and music festivals, militia bands playing in the Botanic Gardens, holiday excursions to the countryside, funerals and weddings, small scandals sweeping through families like tiny squalls, causing turbulence before dying away.

Music filled our lives in many ways. Police bands played on parade days and patriotic occasions. At the dance halls and sports clubs, washboard orchestras and steel bands vied for patronage. Fences and walls were plastered with advertisements for these bands: "Come Hear Eddie's All Stars at BGCC on Old Year's Night!" "Dance to the Enchanting Strains of Dennis Evelyn and His Vibraharp!" You could trip the light fantastic to the brassy rhythms of the Harry Mayers Orchestra or the Demerara Syncopators. You could sway to the soothing sounds of Olga Lopes or the crooning tones of the most recent singing sensation.

Everyone, everywhere seemed to hum or whistle or sing in accompaniment to records playing on the gramophones or the tunes on the radio.

Radios were a fixture in every home and cake shop, every club and rum shop. Ours was a table-top model of dark, polished wood, fifteen inches high or so, with round wooden knobs and a weakly lit yellow dial. The most popular models were Phillips, Zenith and Marconi. Some homes, like my grandparents', had large floor models that were as much a piece of luxurious furniture as they were a radio. Whether we could afford such a model was never an issue – thrift was the guiding principle in our home and, as far as my mother was concerned, the radio was only a marginally acceptable entity.

RADIOS TEMPERED OUR ENERGY AND SLOWED OUR ACTIVITIES. In our home they also created problems since to sit in the rocking chair beside the radio was a privileged post. Except when the seat was occupied by my father, it was available on a first come basis. Many a struggle was precipitated when a concerted dash by two of us for the seat would generate a collision. Might generally prevailed, with the loser limping off, breathing threats and imprecations, sometimes in tears. We loved to

listen to prize fights and Amateur Hour, BBC
news and suspense serials, cricket broadcasts and
Guyana Farewell   western music. Nothing played
a greater part in our lives than
radio. Despite its potential for
generating altercation, listening to the radio was
one of the few pastimes in our home that caused
us to assemble spontaneously to enjoy and discuss
programs, unlike the required appearances we put
in for family prayers, breakfast, lunch, and departure for church on Sunday mornings.

Radio days! Amateur Hour sent us into fits
of laughter and ridicule! The ominous creaking
of an opening door would summon us immediately
to the program Suspense, which would keep us
riveted with horrified expectation, so much so that
the hair rose on the backs of our necks and any
sudden noise outside startled us.

So many of my recollections are tied to radio
broadcasts that THEY FORM A MOSAIC OF LIGHT AND
SOUND AND COLOR, a glowing backdrop that frames
particular times and events forever. Cricket broadcasts, for example, are interwoven in my memory
with the fabric of so many days, weeks, and seasons.

I can summon effortlessly the voices of commentators from cricket grounds worldwide as they chronicle ball by ball, stroke *Radio Days* by stroke, the feats of West Indian cricket teams – at Old Trafford and Lord's, at Sabina Park and Queens Park Oval, at Bridgetown and Bourda, in Bombay and Adelaide. From late morning through the long, hot afternoons in Guyana, the radios in every home and clubhouse, cake shop and rum shop provided a relay of commentary on those cricket matches. The sound followed us, whether on foot or bicycle, through the streets of every town and village, the radio announcer's voice spilling into the sounds of dogs barking, children laughing, bicycle bells ringing, vendors crying their wares.

A tight huddle of men and boys, standing with their bicycles at a street corner, listening to a cricket match on the radio, would spontaneously erupt into elated cheering at a brilliant scoring stroke or a bowled wicket, appreciating both the skill of the batsman and, often as equally, the polished, erudite description by the cricket commentator. The appreciation was often loud and profane:

"Oh rass, man! Yuh heah wha 'e say! 'A square cut dat flash like a sword.' Dat man could sweet talk a camu-

di." And the appreciation was bipartisan. *"Good shot!"* would acclaim an effort from either side – sportsmanship was held in high regard. Many were the altercations, analyses and angry admonitions arising from cricket broadcasts. We all considered ourselves equal in assessing the skill, prowess, and strategy of the captains and the players, the managers and the team selection boards. Arguments about these issues were endless. The scrutiny of each missed catch in the slips, each batsman declared LBW, (leg before wicket), each mishit that yielded a boundary, or an audacious attempt at a stroke, was minute, detailed, contentious. Yet, over and around all the discussions and arguments, the excitement and interest – the seemingly ceaseless flow of the radio voices filled the afternoons of my childhood. *"– begins his long run; shoulders jerking in familiar fashion, he rears up and delivers the ball...;" "– leans into the ball and glides it with elegant, effortless skill...;" "– makes a brilliant, diving catch at silly mid-on to end a splendid hit of thirty-*

five by... ." The voices rose and fell amid the static of many radios, proclaiming and acclaiming a litany of familiar names – Worrell *Radio Days* and Walcott, Valentine and Ramadhin, Gaskin and Pairadeau, batsmen and bowlers, umpires and wicketkeepers, pundits and punsters. A sparkling cascade of commentary spilled and splashed through our lives.

Even cricket at its most entertaining did not exceed the wild excitement generated by the passionate tumult of horse races being announced. Whether we were at the track following the brilliant, rhythmic rise and fall of the silhouettes of jockeys and horses rounding a distant bend, or if we were placing a bet illegally at a rum shop, or just bicycling to some appointment, THE RISING, EXCITED VOICE OF THE UBIQUITOUS RADIOS BLARING INTO THE AFTERNOON WOULD SEIZE OUR ATTENTION. *"And they're off!"* was calculated to stop everyone in their tracks and freeze conversations in mid-sentence as we strained to catch the frenzied, tumultuous accounts of the action. *"They're coming into the homestretch with Dancing Girl drifting out from the rails... ,"* the voice excited, rising, insistent.

"On the inside, Eruption is beginning to make his

Guyana Farewell   *move...they are neck and neck*

coming down the stretch!"

Every listener would be caught up in the pulsing, staccato description. I can see my father, his face flushed, his eyes intense, leaning forward. The high-pitched torrent of words came spilling from the open windows of houses. Pedestrians stopped to listen, loudly exhorting their favorites. Shopkeepers paused in mid-transaction, sugar dribbling heedlessly into the scales, the horses filling their imaginations with the thunder of hooves and the frenzied flailings of jockeys astride straining, perspiring steeds. Moments later, the race over and life, released from the drama, resumed, vendors would complete their sales, bicycles would start moving, and pedestrians would walk onward as the radio voices died away.

The prize fights at Madison Square Garden, broadcast on the American Armed Forces Radio, thrilled and excited my brothers and me more than any program. Whether it was our local pursuit of amateur boxing, our need for heroes, or the unadulterated savagery of the action, these fights, especially the heavyweight championship contests, were unforgettable events for us.

Radio Days

The conditions under which we listened enhanced the experience enormously. The difference in time between the United States and British Guiana meant that these contests, which started at 10:00 or 11:00 p.m., would be heard at home as late as 1:00 or 2:00 a.m. My mother's disapproval of most radio programs, coupled with the nature of prize fights, meant that we had to listen clandestinely, stealing from our beds cautiously to huddle around the radio in the after-midnight darkness. As the faint light of the radio dial gleamed in our eyes, someone would patiently turn the knob searching for the radio transmission. RECEPTION WAS FAINT, INTERMITTENT. The need to keep the volume low to avoid alerting our mother created a cabal of conspirers whispering suggestions, craning necks and straining ears to recognize the broadcast first. How thrilling to finally hear, after interminable minutes of tuning and twiddling, the stentorian tones of the referee at

Madison Square Garden announcing the fighters!
We shivered with excitement and anticipation until

Guyana Farewell the bell for the first round
clanged. Too often, the trans-
mission would fade away into
static, leaving us frantic. Occasionally, one of us
would have to be cautioned angrily when, carried
away by the frantic blow-by-blow description, we
began throwing punches wildly or started exhorting
our favored pugilist too loudly – Joe Louis, Billy
Conn, Rocky Graziano, Tony Zale, Randy Turpin
and, of course, the hated Max Schmeling. The
names ring like bells in my memory, triggering recollections of famous contests that transported us
from the warm, early morning darkness of the little
room to the brilliant spotlights and raucous tumult
of ringside, thousands of miles and light years of
reality away.

War over the Airwaves And then, of course,
there were the war years and the BBC news broadcasts. Years later I would read historic accounts
of people who suffered through World War II in
Europe and Asia – how they waited desperately for
crucial, often life-or-death British Broadcasting

Corporation transmissions. I marveled then at our innocence and obliviousness. Too young to comprehend the significance of *Radio Days* the events tearing the fabric of nations and empires apart – cocooned in the sleepy backwater of an insignificant colony and preoccupied with the rituals, tribulations and joys of childhood – we hovered on the periphery of adults as they listened with varying degrees of shock, trepidation, dismay, defiance and triumph to the BBC radio broadcasters with their calm, measured reporting of World War II. Nevertheless, six years of war and its accompanying propaganda inevitably permeated and indelibly affected our consciousness. PERHAPS, MORE THAN ANY SINGLE EVENT, THE PURSUIT AND CRIPPLING OF THE GERMAN BATTLESHIP GRAF SPEE CAPTURED OUR IMAGINATIONS.

In December, 1939, when these events occurred, I had just turned five. I don't know if, as a five-year old, I actually followed the progress of the dramatic engagement in the South Atlantic. Still, the vividness of the recollection is difficult to banish – with its images of sleek, gray British cruis ers cleaving the turbulent waters in relentless pursuit of the German pocket battleship that had sunk

so many merchant ships. Like the flotsam of those torpedoed ships, names rise to the surface of my mind – H.M.S. Hood, Ajax, Exeter, Montevideo. Perhaps it was the jubilation of the adults that marked the occasion unforgettably or the voice of my grandfather recounting the affair and explaining their joy to us as children. My memories of the wartime broadcasts are inextricably tied to the sounds of the presentations themselves: the "pip...pip...pip" preceding, *"This is the BBC,"* and the sound of British voices, chronicling the unfolding drama of World War II.

Amateur Hour Every Sunday afternoon we settled down around the radio in delighted anticipation of Amateur Hour, a favorite of everyone. After several auditions, the participants won the opportunity to perform on Radio Demerara, "the voice of Guiana." Most of the contestants were singers, with an occasional instrumental solo and an infrequent comedian. The featured singers were generally self-tutored. They might choose a song from the current hit parade, a traditional favorite from a light opera or a Broadway musical or, less frequently, a calypso, a hymn or a folksong, usually British. Favorites were: "Oh Danny Boy," "A Tree," and "Some Enchanted Evening." Most performers chose a popular version of a song they felt most suited their style and attempted to emulate the original recording. With little access to recording equipment, the contestants could only predict their own success by soliciting the opinions of friends or by listening to themselves. IT WAS NOT A METHOD CALCULATED TO BE AN ACCURATE BAROM- ETER and the results provided considerable enter- tainment for a keenly anticipatory audience.

"And now, we give you Mr. Dennis Ramharry, singing the lovely ballad..." The fulsome tones of a popular radio personality announcing the first con- testant would hardly have died away when an over- anxious singer would launch into an off-key rendi- tion of "Oh Danny Boy," only to stop confusedly, perhaps at the signal of the accompanist, then com- mence once more, resolutely on key. This occa- sioned much giggling from the listeners, but if the

singer continued and brought the performance to a successful conclusion, there would be the friendly

Guyana Farewell sounds of approbation: *"Oh, Rab, mahn! 'e mek a good try!"* followed by a round of applause from the studio audience. An aspiring calypso singer might be next, usually confining his efforts to a well-known selection with a strong rhythmic beat, thereby reducing the need for much individuality. Occasionally, however, some confident young calypso singer, assured by friends of the originality of his compositions and the verve of his performances, appeared on the program and sent listeners into paroxysms of laughter with his efforts.

A highlight of Amateur Hour was the announcer's gong used to terminate disastrous performances. Although the gong was invoked infrequently in order to encourage the flow of performers, ITS THREAT WAS SUFFICIENT TO TITILLATE THE EXPECTANT RADIO AUDIENCE.

Even though most listeners could usually determine fairly quickly when the gong was likely to be struck by the announcer, the sharpness and finality of the sound always startled everyone into laughter and animated comments.

It was the animated conversations and exchanges among the coun-

trywide audience that the Amateur Hour generated, more than any other single factor, which ensured its longevity. One always knew someone who knew a contestant or the musical selection might be a current favorite we had all tried to render privately, or there was some characteristic of the performer that provoked interest.

Usually the contestants were asked what they did for a living and their answers provided an important clue to their social standing. That information, together with their manner of speaking, helped to establish in the minds of the audience a distinct picture and profile. In general, contestants came from humble circumstances. This was due to the nature of society in a small colony with powerful Victorian traditions, constraints and inhibitions. The better educated a person was and the more substantive his employment – the higher his status, essentially – the less likely a person was to risk exposing an aspiration to be something as frivolous

as a popular singer or performer. The introductory
questioning having been completed, the contestant

Guyana Farewell was asked for his or her selection. The answer might be
timidly whispered, causing the
radio announcer to ask again. Another time, the
response might be delivered in ringing tones, sending a message that this performer was not nervous.
Everyone tittered. The preliminary chords played
on the piano by the accompanist sounded, the
aspiring singer might launch resolutely into a barely
recognizable "Ave Maria," agonizingly off key. We
waited breathlessly. Would he start again? Would
the accompanist stop? "Bing-g-g-g!" The sound of
the gong startled everyone. The performer stopped
abruptly in mid-note, everyone laughed heartily as
the mortified contestant was escorted off, and the
announcer made sympathetic noises. More often,
the performance would be satisfactory, if unin-
spired. Yet, several of our most successful popular
singers launched their careers on Amateur Hour
and their accomplishments encouraged a steady
flow of poets, calypsonians, crooners and instru-
mentalists through the years.

I set out for my first day of secondary school on a September morning in 1947, accompanied by my older brother Ronald. The early morning sun shone on a small 12-year-old boy dressed in a new school uniform: white shirt, short pleated khaki trousers, a school tie with yellow, black and red stripes, head crowned with a large pith helmet with a badge that matched the tie.

Everything I wore was new and itchy but it was the hat, which had an adjustable inner head-band, that caused me the most discomfort. PITH HELMETS, WITH THEIR LARGE BRIMS, WERE A RIDICU-LOUS REQUIREMENT FOR SMALL BOYS. Relays of stick-thin boys in their early teens, crowned by this oversized headgear, were a familiar early morning sight bicycling along Brickdam, and in later years along Camp Street after Queens College was relocated to a large new building.

In those days, Queens College was where it had been for many years, at the corner of Brickdam and Vlissingen Roads, four or five blocks from our home on Robb Street. Ronald and I walked down Oronoque Street for three blocks, crossed a six-foot-wide water-filled trench by balancing on a pipe that bridged it, turned left along the opposite bank and, after about fifty yards, turned right across a small, wooden footbridge. We then followed a narrow footpath between playing fields to Brickdam. Directly across that street were wide-open iron gates in a high hedge, framing the entrance to the large four-story mansion that was the main building of Queens College.

On that first day as I sat quietly at my desk, surrounded by mostly new and uncertain classmates, awaiting the arrival of our first teacher, uncertainty, apprehension, trepidation engulfed me. Two of my brothers had preceded me at Queens College and, before them, an uncle, so I was steeped in the traditions of the school. Still, the actual fact of being there was overwhelming. How much more

Guyana Farewell

so it must have been for others, without a similar background, to find themselves on their first day at the school that represented the epitome of academic arrival in our small British colony.

It was a familiar setting for those students who lived in Georgetown, but for the "country boys," graduates of schools in places like New Amsterdam, Rose Hall, Mahaica, Essequibo and Mackenzie, it must have been a shock of acculturation!

Many of the "country boys" group were Indians. Much of the countryside of sugar plantations, rice fields and villages of small merchants was the province of the descendants of indentured servants brought from India in the nineteenth century to work on the plantations. How little we knew of each other then and how little we learned of each other's lives before Queens.

As we sat at our small battered wooden desks with their inkwells and array of initials carved by predecessors, we listened to the roster called alphabetically by the form master, acknowledged our names and sized each other up surreptitiously, speculating on each other's backgrounds and capabilities. All we knew of each other *Upper School* was that most of us had won scholarships in the colony-wide, competitive examinations for admission to Queens College.

The Freedom of Privilege On subsequent mornings during my first year at Queens, while riding my bike to school, I remember reflecting on the extraordinary difference in my circumstances from the previous year in elementary school. Then, I had thought of myself as a child and it seemed as if life was shuttered by an interminable round of school, homework, private lessons, punishment, chores and duty.

At Queens, despite the regimen of classes, homework and discipline, windows had opened for me, revealing vistas of freedom and potential accomplishment. After-school sports replaced the terrible anxiety I had about after-school lessons. THE NOVELTY OF OWNING TEXTBOOKS THAT COULD BE TAKEN HOME AND PERUSED AT MY LEISURE WAS EXHILARATING. Even more wonderful was the school's library, in a room of its own, with its many shelves of books waiting to be read.

Guyana Farewell   To arrive at school and mingle with my new colleagues before classes, enjoying a sense of status and imagined consequence as we regaled each other with the previous day's highlights – incidents in classes, amusing or notable comments by one of the masters, accomplishments on the fields of sport – was an ambiance so different, so exotic, that for much of that first year I felt an uncharacteristic euphoria.

It is difficult to convey the enormous shift in perspective, atmosphere and status that qualifying for admission and entering Queens College generated for me. The metamorphosis from the careful constraints of elementary school to the greater freedom of my new school began at about age ten. Identified by the school principal as academically capable of achieving the standards set for the annual competitive examination for scholarships to enter the government high schools, I WAS REQUIRED BY MY PARENTS TO BEGIN A REGIMEN OF AFTER-SCHOOL TUTORING. This regimen culminated in sitting for the examination on two occasions, first in our eleventh year and again the following year. If we were successful in attaining *Upper School* the highest marks, we won one of a small number of spe-cial scholarships that allowed us to enroll in one of the two government secondary schools – Queens College or Bishops High School – in September of our 12th year.

I won one of these scholarships by attaining higher marks than most of those competing. I have no recollection of the content of that examination, but it probably included the requisite arithmetic, English and essay writing that constituted the core of our colonial education in elementary school. But I do remember, and have never forgotten, how scared I was when, escorted by my sister, Sheila, I set out for the school site I had been assigned to, and the realization dawned that, unless I was successful, I would not be able to join my older brothers at Queens.

Waiting at my desk flanked by rows of neatly dressed boys and girls, I remember searching, unsuccessfully, for a familiar face among the teachers and principals appointed as monitors. Before me, turned face down on the desk, was the first

Guyana Farewell part of the examination and, on the command to commence working, I picked it up with trembling fingers, turned it over and stared blindly at it for a few seconds. I seemed to be the only one stricken by doubts. Everyone else was bending industriously over their work and the soft sound of pencil on paper, the quiet footsteps of the monitors and an occasional bicycle bell from the street were the only intruders on the stillness.

Completing that examination successfully ushered me into a new world.

Something as simple as a separate classroom was a novelty after the open space and clamor of elementary school. Attending Queens College meant that we were considered special. It ensured that we would have a rigorous education and be expected to continue the school's long and cherished tradition of scholarship, sportsmanship, and professional achievement.

As students there, we gained access to privileges and facilities, teaching and coaching that

enabled us, if we took advantage of it all, to compete successfully in whatever field of study, area of
professional occupation and
region of the world we elect-
ed. The opportunities that we
considered special in that
small, impoverished British
colony seem, in retrospect, so limited and inconse-
quential that it is difficult to conceive how important they were to us, our families and the society.

The Reluctant Scholar For the next six years,
school was to be the dominant factor in my life.
I was not a good student. I found the work tedious,
the teachers autocratic, uninspiring and humorless, the homework burdensome and the regimen
depressing. I looked forward with great anticipation
to the mid-morning and midday breaks. I hated
Latin from the outset and disliked the master, Mr.
Taitt. Paradoxically I found myself intrigued by
Homer's *Iliad* and *Odyssey* and Virgil's *Aeneid* and,
therefore, I was willing to struggle with my declen-
sions. I came to hate math in the middle grades,
baffled particularly by geometry and the insuffer-
able, unsympathetic teacher, Mr. Chunilall, with

his inadequate mumbled explanations.

French was tolerable for me until I had to

endure the ministrations of my fourth form teacher, Mr. Larte, and his sarcastic deprecation of my efforts at taking French dictation. There was something partly appealing to me, however, about his sardonic style and the accuracy with which he could throw a piece of chalk at an inattentive or dozing student. Science, and, in particular, chemistry seemed a muddle of test tubes and Bunsen burners filled with useless fuming substances that had to be recorded endlessly.

English, history and geography offered the only surcease from the monotony. Even there, with few exceptions, I FOUND THE TEACHING TO BE PEDESTRIAN. One teacher in particular, Miss Bragg, was as dry as dust and a humorless autocrat who insisted that she be addressed as Miss instead of Mrs. Bragg. She made geography, a potentially interesting subject, miserably mundane.

I received my first dose of corporal punishment at Queens when the paper slug propelled from a rubber band I was using hit Norman

Beaton, sitting in the front row, on the back of his head with a resounding splat. It made him cry and I, sick with remorse, owned *Upper School* up to the dastardly act. I was given six of the best on my backside with a flexible bamboo cane by the principal, Mr. Beckles. His enthusiastic execution of this duty, though acutely painful to me physically, was considerably less so than his verbal castigation of my behavior in the privacy of his office. Beaton forgave me, even congratulating me on my accuracy, but I abandoned rubber band activity thereafter.

Discipline was taken seriously by adults. Punishments included after-school detention; submission of endless written repetitions of such sentences as, "I will refrain from chattering in class," or loftier sentiments in Latin; early morning weeding in the garden, and, of course, a "spare the rod, spoil the child" genuflection. But there were many small pleasures and accomplishments that tempered my experience at Queens, some so quaint in retrospect that laughter wells up when I contemplate them.

We read British books about schoolboy escapades, particularly of a fat bespectacled boy at boarding school, Billy Bunter, who was always the butt of his schoolmates' jokes. We imitated his

ridiculous expressions of outrage, adopted his mannerisms and identified with his mishaps and occasional victories. At mid-morning breaks, we jostled for service in the "tuck shop" to purchase tennis rolls, coconut buns, and lemonade with our meager allowances. Convinced of our sophistication now that we had achieved the eminence of Queens, WE ENGAGED IN LOFTY DISCUSSION OF ESOTERIC SUBJECTS — TOSSING AROUND NEW LATIN OR FRENCH EXPRESSIONS WE HAD ENCOUNTERED IN OUR CLASSES — and struck poses of characters recognizable from books we had read or copied from upperclassmen.

Only in the upper fourth form could you begin wearing long trousers, which provided a clear delineation between the seniors and the insignificant second, third and lower fourth-formers. The school prefects — upperclassmen with authority to see that rules were observed — could reprimand, punish with after-school detention and report more serious offenses to the staff. Some of the prefects

were relaxed about their responsibilities, and preferred to advise and caution rather than meting
out immediate punishment. *Upper School*
Other more officious prefects
were uniformly detested for
their enthusiastic observance of certain rules that
were often flouted, especially the rule that school
uniforms should be properly worn to and from
school. To be cited by one of these prefects for a tie
that was not neatly knotted or an unnoticed shirt-
tail hanging out was not uncommon. Most likely
of these violations was to be caught without your
pith helmet – or "bughouse," as we used to call it –
on your head, since the helmets were uniformly
disliked, both for their unwieldiness and because
they provided a target for the ridicule and occasional missiles of local ruffians.

All students at Queens during the years
I was there were assigned to one of four and, later,
six houses. Each house was named in honor of a
renowned former principal, teacher or other significant graduate, but was also designated by a letter
of the alphabet for brevity and assigned a color.
A student's school tie, in addition to carrying the

school's colors of yellow and black, incorporated the color of his house. Each was headed by a house master, usually a senior teacher. Most administrative duties, though, were carried out by a student house captain, assisted by deputies.

To be appointed house captain was a considerable honor and required that the appointee show significant athletic and academic achievement, with somewhat more emphasis on the athletic prowess. Such prowess was often equated with leadership potential, a characteristic highly prized by the college. Houses competed against each other, primarily in sports.

Tradition required that successive family members attending Queens be assigned to the same house. My family was in Percival or A House with red as its color. I was enormously proud of the affiliation and determined to somehow uphold its traditions and contribute to its successes. As early as I can recollect, Sports Day at Queens was a wonderful occasion because I could watch my older brothers compete and bask in the reflected glory of their accomplishments. Nothing was more wonderful than being able to say *"That's my brother!"* as an older sibling accomplished some spectacular athletic feat while you watched *Upper School* proudly in the company of friends and strangers.

Houses were the focus of all activity outside the classroom. At house meetings held every morning, various school announcements were made by the house captain in which activities were delineated, achievements acknowledged and individual recognition assigned. In my first two years at Queens, certain daily and weekly events were especially important to newcomers. In particular, tryouts for intramural sports teams at the beginning of the cricket, soccer and field hockey seasons were significant. Each week, the captains of the teams would post a list of those who would represent each house in that week's sports activities.

THE FIRST TIME I SAW MY NAME ON THE LIST, THE BURST OF PRIDE I EXPERIENCED WAS OVERWHELMING.

The congratulations that day from my classmates and the more senior house members are my first memory of receiving unadulterated praise. To a middle child in a family of six, in which exceptional academic and athletic accomplishment was expected and routine, the unaccustomed recognition and

Guyana Farewell

acclaim was indescribable.

At Queens, the only thing more significant than the recognition of your classmates was the approving notice of an upperclassman. To be singled out in passing by a remark as casual as *"Good show, young Bacchus,"* or to have my older brother pass on the information that my name had been mentioned approvingly in some upperclassman's conversation, was the zenith of achievement for me. Awards, athletic, academic or other, were the school's and the society's symbols, but for them to be fully significant, they had to be accompanied by the recognition of the student body. On that morning, I truly felt I had arrived.

Sports Day was a very important annual event at Queens College. It could just as easily have been called Family Day – it was the occasion on which the students' families came together under the auspices of the school for a full afternoon of track and field activities, at the same time that the alumni gathered to reminisce and revel. The focus of the activity was the annual athletic competition among the College Houses. Sports Day was held, usually, at the grounds of the *Upper School* Georgetown Cricket Club, a sports field with several large sheltered stands, or bleachers, and a main clubhouse. The grounds were encircled by high fences of corrugated zinc sheets, painted red and plastered with advertising posters, as well as a water-filled trench.

For weeks before, we all trained assiduously at our particular events. Since I intended to qualify for competition in the track events, I would rise in the early morning, summoned by crowing cocks, don my shirt, shorts and sneakers and, careful not to awaken the family, tiptoe through the hall and down the backstairs. Then, away down New Garden Street I ran, across Lamaha to Vlissingen Road. Past white picket fences and flowering gardens, along the rails by the Demerara Cricket Club, down an avenue of large, blooming flamboyant trees, under which the ground was sprinkled with the bright-red, fallen blossoms. I MIGHT SEE A FLASH OF YELLOW AND BLACK AND THE BLUR OF WINGS THAT PRECEDED THE CHARACTERISTIC SONG OF A

KISKADEE as I ran along the straight asphalt stretch of road by the rifle range.

Guyana Farewell   The smell of the ocean and the faint sound of waves intensified as I reached the familiar upward incline to the seashore and the long road that paralleled the seawall. Sometimes, when the tide was out, the rank smell of the mud flats would permeate the air, but mostly I remember the early morning sunshine as I ran, the soft, balmy breeze, the sound of the waves and the distant smoke plume from a ship at the river's entrance.

As I returned home, I passed the Indian Cricket Club and the parade ground, turned left along Lamaha Street and the canal, occasionally essaying a different street. ALL WAS STILL IN THE EARLY SUNSHINE, BEFORE THE BICYCLES AND DONKEY CARTS ARRIVED ON THE WAY TO THE MARKETS. I might pass a market lady, late and hurrying, her huge basket of fruit or vegetables resting atop a donut roll of cloth on a motionless head, her smoothly rhythmic movement of hips, torso and legs creating a sense of effortless gliding.

After school, we would repair to the playing

fields and hurdle or high jump or pole vault or
do interval running. We wore running shoes with
spikes, basic black models *Upper School*
produced cheaply by Bata, a
British company, and sold at
one of the few department stores in Georgetown.
My father somehow always managed to find the
money to buy us the equipment we needed for
athletic pursuits – track shoes, soccer boots, cricket
bats, hockey sticks, and innumerable pairs of
cheap sneakers. All of this precious equipment had
to be cared for, cleaned, polished or greased. Our
sneakers, ridiculously known as "yachting shoes,"
were washed regularly, layered with "whitening"
and set out to dry in the sun.

As Sports Day approached, there would be a
rising swell of speculation, rumors and prognostica-
tion about the respective prospects of the various
houses. Intense assessments of the athletes based on
observing their form during practices or their previous record would be exchanged in the inevitable
groups of students around the school grounds. In
particular, among the youngest students who were
newcomers to the affair, there was constant specula-

tion about the ability of their classmates who would compete in the lowest category, the under13 group.

Guyana Farewell

Preliminary heats were run and finally, the list of competitors in each event in each age group – under13, under15, under17 and Open – would be posted on the bulletin boards of each of the houses.

We lived only two blocks away from the sports ground and, before I became a student at Queens and could participate in Sports Day, I would sit on our front steps and watch the crowds of fans heading there for the many regular sports events – cricket, cycle races, football, soccer games. On Sports Day my excitement was unbounded. I was given a note to the principal of my school requesting that I be excused from the afternoon session to allow me to attend the event. I hurried home from school at lunch time to change my clothes and wait impatiently for my sister and her friends to get ready. Sitting on the steps, wriggling with impatience, I acknowledged the greetings of family friends as they passed and, with barely concealed pride, fielded their queries about the prospects of my brothers' success.

Finally, we set out, my sister and her friends, all smartly dressed, talking animatedly. I held the hand of my younger brother, *Upper School* David, and tried to refrain from skipping or hopping with joy. In the few photographs taken of those days, the serious, slightly suspicious demeanor I offered to the camera amuses but does not really surprise me. I doubt whether I was fully conscious of the photo-taking as anything more than an intrusion into the childish world of my thoughts and imagination. I had little time for smiling and posturing for adults. Their lives were so distant from my comprehension and of so little concern that I could have been on a different planet.

Very seldom did my parents participate in our childhood activities. MY FATHER OPERATED ON THE FRINGES OF MY LIFE, always there, but in much the same way as the roof of the house or the regularity of the seasons. I might look up in a moment of respite during a fiercely contested soccer game to see him standing next to his bicycle on the street by the sports field, watching. Yet, before the game was over, he would have departed. On another occasion, he could be seen chatting with an acquaintance as they appraised the performance of

one of their children in a cricket match, but rarely would he volunteer a comment on our ability.

I could not help but recognize as time went on that the prowess of Ronald was a source of considerable pride to him. I would watch my father as he acknowledged the compliments of a stranger or an acquaintance on some especially brilliant bit of batting in a cricket match or the sudden, explosive acceleration that left Ronald open to score a goal in soccer or field hockey. I found it difficult to reconcile that charming, smiling individual accepting praise so graciously, with the normally serious, quiet and occasionally exasperated demeanor of my father.

On the morning of Sports Day, our excitement was palpable. Perhaps, on the evening before, my father might have a masseur come to the house to give us a massage. Lying on the bed being tugged and pummeled, rubbed and thumped into a limp heap, my mind would be flooded with memories of previous Sports Days. I would recall my oldest brother, Patrick, at the peak of a pole-vaulting effort, twisting gracefully in the air to surmount the cross bar, dropping into the *Upper School* sawdust pit and turning casually to catch the thin, bamboo pole he had used. Or I would remember him when he surged over the hurdles as he battled head-to-head with a good friend and tough rival to reach the tape first. Memories fast-forwarded through my brain as I remembered Ronald as he burst from the starting holes and accelerated in a blur of knees and arms, pulling away to win the 100-yard dash. Or I would see Ronald coming from behind in a burst of speed to match an opponent stride for stride down the final stretch to the tape, finally beating him with a desperate lunge, all to the frantic exhortations of his House members. HOW THE ZINC WALLS OF THE SPORTS GROUND WOULD ECHO AGAIN AND AGAIN with the applause of schoolboys, schoolmasters, families, admirers and alumni!

In the bright sunshine, house banners flutter while the bright frocks of female relatives and the girls from our sister school, Bishops High, create splashes of color among the drab white shirts and

khaki uniforms of the school body. Happy laughter
and animated voices fill the stands where families

Guyana Farewell   and friends gossip and reminisce, while they share the con-
tents of heavy picnic baskets.
The baskets are filled with patties and pinetarts,
and piles of neatly cut triangles of sandwiches –
ham and cheese and chicken, ground and seasoned
with pepper sauce and spices – carefully wrapped
in damp, muslin cloths to keep them fresh. The
baskets are the source of intense interest to the ever-
hungry students. Pitchers of mauby and ginger
beer, frosted on the outside, tinkle with ice cubes as
they are passed from hand to hand. Less frequently,
a bottle of rum might be passed, to be mixed
with ginger ale, soda and coca-cola, and poured
over ice. The fragrant smell of the rum lingers softly
in the air, barely noticeable amid the powder and
perfume of the women.

The sports field, its carefully manicured grass
presenting a green expanse, is cluttered with officials and sprinkled with the accouterments of an
athletic contest – rows of white painted hurdles, the
pole vault and high jump uprights bordered by the

pale yellow of their sawdust pits, and tiny, multi-colored flags staked at regular intervals to delineate the track. The focus of atten- *Upper School* tion between athletic events is a large, white tea-tent where dignitaries and select members of the college staff, ensconced at tables covered with white linen, are served tea and sandwiches.

The scene floats like a faintly seen reflection in the quiet pond of my memory. IT IS ALWAYS SUNLIT AND NO ONE GROWS OLDER.

I suppose I remember Sports Day so vividly because in some way it epitomizes the quality of life then, the things that were important, the sense of tradition and continuity, the handing down from generation to generation. Nostalgia is the transformation of the past into the perfect.

A Bicycle Culture

Everyone rode bicycles – that is, everyone who could afford to purchase a new or used one. Everyone else walked or rode the rickety buses. If your bike was being repaired, was borrowed or stolen, you might pop over to a friend's house to borrow one or to solicit a "tow." Being towed was the term for riding on the cross bar, carrier or handle of someone's bicycle. The request, "Tow me to school!" was a common one.

Bicycle Etiquette   Bicycles were so intrinsic a part of the culture in Guyana when I was growing up that it is impossible to remember a scene in which they did not constitute a prop, backdrop, framework or primary focus. Whether going to work or school, rushing to after school activities, leisurely socializing with friends, "taking the air" by the sea or riding slowly by the home of one's current object of affection, bicycles dominated other means of conveyance. In our small society, bicycle-riding etiquette was well established and carefully observed. IT WAS SHOCKING FOR A FEMALE TO RIDE A MAN'S BICYCLE – ONE WITH A CROSSBAR – SINCE IT WAS NECESSARY TO THROW ONE'S LEG OVER THE SADDLE TO MOUNT. Because dresses were *de rigeur*, such behavior demonstrated a lack of modesty. Being "towed" on the crossbar of a man's bicycle was not permissible for a female unless the male was a relative, or some understanding had been reached by the respective families concerning the relationship. How quickly gossip would circulate and how soon a reprimand would be forthcoming!

Correct bicycle procedures, established and enforced by the constabulary, required riding on the proper side of the street, stopping at stop signs and signaling to indicate one was turning. A bicycle license – a small metal plate with a number – was issued annually for a fee and had to be displayed correctly. Failing to have a bicycle bell, front and rear brakes that functioned properly or a lighted bicycle lamp after dark subjected one to a summons

by any police officer and an appearance in court resulting, usually, in a fine. IT IS DIFFI-CULT TO CONVEY THE APPREHENSIVENESS OF A TEENAGER OR YOUNG ADULT TRYING TO SNEAK HOME AFTER DARK ON A BICYCLE WITH A DEFECTIVE LAMP. You knew that being caught by a constable posted at a street corner or patrolling on a bike would pre-cipitate several unpleasant things. Your brakes, bell and license would be checked, you would have to appear in court to the dismay of your parents, and your own sense of shame would compound as you mingled with miscreants and criminals.

The system of monitoring bicycling procedure was, however, as prone to personal influence as any devised by humans. My younger brother, Maxey, was horrified at being caught one evening riding with a lamp that didn't work. He stammered out a false name – John Smith – to the constable. Since his ethnic origin was obvious to the officer and the name unlikely, he was about to be taken off to the lock-up for compounding his transgression by making a false statement. A neighbor passed by, recognized him and stopped. He asked the constable if he was aware who the young man's father was and suggested carefully that a strict warning might be more appropriate. Maxey, suitably ashamed, was sent off with his ears ringing from the officer's reprimand, though perhaps more bothered by the mild reproof from our neighbor.

Bicycle service and repair at the ubiquitous hole-in-the-wall bicycle shops were a regular part of life. These little establishments were often no more than a narrow space between two larger buildings into which had been crowded a jumble of paraphernalia. Sheltered by old zinc sheets or a rickety plywood roof, the main equipment was often a rope or chain hanging from a beam on which a bicycle could be suspended for attention. Usually a one-man operation, it would be jammed with cannibalized bikes and stocked with patching kits and old and new bicycle tires and tubes. Cardboard boxes filled with nuts and screws rested among a clutter of parts – lights, bells, brakepads, pedals, saddles, carriers, sprockets, old license plates, wheels and handles. Tires, inner tubes, lamps and bells needed constant examination or replacement, since theft of these items was frequent. Bicycle theft was a serious offense. Much of police work involved pursuing bicycle thieves, tracking down stolen bikes and responding to citizens' complaints. Bicycle accidents never failed to attract an interested group of onlookers.

The Promenade Promenading on bicycles along the coast road by the seawall was a social ritual participated in by everyone local to Georgetown, and by many visitors as well. This stone wall, four feet high and at least as wide, was built by the early Dutch colonists to prevent the sea from engulfing early settlements at high tide. It ran along the shore from the mouth of the Demerara River for several miles northwards. The wall looked out across an expanse of brown sand to the sea – coffee-colored from silt brought down by the river – and a distant horizon where the masts of fishing boats and the smoke rising from the funnels of steamers and freighters were often visible.

Landward, the terrain sloped downward and

the view was of open, uncultivated fields that adjoined the playing fields of various sports and the rifle range of the militia. This  area formed a green belt, about a mile wide, between the coast road and Lamaha Street where the rows of small, white-painted wooden houses commenced. After the road from town converged with the coast road, the seawall widened into a broad promenade with a bathhouse and rows of curved-backed slatted wooden benches.

Facing the promenade on the landward side was a classic circular bandstand within an expanse of greensward bordered by a low, white picket fence. Its ornamental iron railings painted black and its red conical roof with decorative cast-iron fringes were maintained in pristine condition by the Public Works Department. HERE THE MILITIA BAND GAVE WEEKLY CONCERTS ON SUNDAY AFTER NOONS AND FAMILIES GATHERED TO TAKE THE AIR, GOSSIP AND APPLAUD THE PERFORMANCES. The program was fairly varied, with classical selections, military marches and an occasional lighter offering.

All the seats at the bandstand were usually taken by older people. Children played restrainedly

Guyana Farewell nearby, in respect of their smart Sunday outfits. Groups of teenage boys and girls sauntered self-consciously in separate groups, giggling and flirting, and young couples courted under the watchful scrutiny of relatives. MOST AFTERNOONS, EXCEPT WHEN IT RAINED, THE SEAWALL WAS A GATHERING PLACE, A RENDEZVOUS, WITNESS TO A SLOW PROMENADE OF BICYCLISTS, ANXIOUS TO SEE AND BE SEEN.

On weekends, groups of bicyclists made excursions to villages along the coast, riding as far as ten or fifteen miles with their picnic baskets and sports equipment loaded on their bikes. The hot tropical sun poured down on the flat landscape, with its luxuriant green of rice paddies and red roads bordered by ditches half-filled with water.

Along the route of these excursions, villages of ramshackle, one-story wooden houses and dilapidated shops with corrugated zinc roofs bustled with shopkeepers and roadside vendors carrying their baskets of fruits and vegetables. Everything reverberated with the frenzied barking of stray dogs, the clamor of blaring radios, the ringing of bicycle bells and the shouts of children. *A Bicycle Culture*

There was little need to worry about motor cars since only a small portion of the population owned them. More dangerous were the heavily laden wooden buses that traveled between the capital and the villages along the coastal road. The road was made of crushed gravel and red sand compressed by heavy rollers into a moderately smooth surface. Parallel concrete strips, laid down at the width of motorized vehicle wheels, ran down the middle of the road.

Bicyclists riding on these strips gave way periodically to speeding buses and lorries with their imperious, bugling horns and insouciant drivers. Since the edges of the roads were often in a state of disrepair, the transfer from concrete strips to gravel surface had to be negotiated with care, occasioning hilarity, depending on the state of the road and the skill of the riders. Streams of imprecations were often directed at the bus drivers and their jeering, gesticulating passengers.

The Race Is On Bicycle racing was a natural

outgrowth of the fact that bicycles were the primary means of transportation. The bicycle excursions to

the countryside often turned into road races, and the sight of a pumping, perspiring group of cyclists whizzing along the coastal road was not uncommon on weekends. The bicycles used for racing were a curious mix of stripped-down models and lighter but standard frames reworked in one of the many bicycle repair shops. In part this was preparation for the semi-annual cycle races organized by the Guyana Cycling Authority.

These tournaments were advertised with great fanfare weeks in advance of the two- or three-day event. The grounds of a local cricket club was the usual site. Large enough to permit the preparation of a quarter-mile oval track, the club grounds were enclosed by high fences of corrugated zinc and had bleachers and stands that could accommodate a large crowd. Access without tickets was restricted by a ten-foot wide trench filled with water that prevented all but the most enterprising from scaling the fences. The bike-racing track was similar in appearance to any athletic field for footracing, except that the surface of the track was rolled and compressed to reduce slipping on the surface during the tighter turns. *A Bicycle Culture*

For weeks prior to the tournament, the local bicycle clubs trained assiduously on the city streets, the coastal roads and the road that ran inland parallel to the river. Other groups from the outlying villages and from further away across the Berbice and Essequibo Rivers trained throughout the year in their attempts to seize dominance from the town clubs. Rumors of dynamic newcomers to the cycling scene drifted through conversations. Local newspapers – *The Argosy, The Daily Chronicle, The Daily Graphic* – speculated on the prospects, form and records of the reigning champions. I remember how my brothers and I and our friends organized local meetings on our block. We raced wildly along the streets, careening precariously around corners, finishing in bursts of speed, hands thrown in the air triumphantly in passionate emulation of our heroes. The scar on the inside of my left wrist is a memento of those days. I failed to navigate one such turn successfully and crashed into the ditch and fence.

During the early years, the bicycle races were generally limited to local riders. As the organizers

became more effective, and the prowess of local riders became greater and gate receipts grew, invitations were issued to champions from the near-by islands of Barbados and Trinidad. Later, teams from Venezuela became occasional participants and, on one or two occasions, cyclists from Italy and one from the U.S.A. sent local fans into a frenzy of delight and anticipation. On opening day, the excitement would be intense. The stands, jammed with excited fans, seemed to sag and rock precariously. The lines to cross the narrow, creaky wooden bridges to the entrances were long and animated.

Local characters engaged in loud, jeering exchanges about the prospects of rival teams. In the least expensive bleachers, shouting, swearing fans would indulge freely in various brands of Demerara rum in pint bottles with gaudy labels. It was not uncommon to see an overexcited drunk fall out of one of the stands and be carted away. In the Pavilion, as the best accommodation was called, the better class would imbibe in a more genteel man-

ner, favoring ice-filled glasses of rum with ginger
ale or soda, served by white-jacketed waiters. Whis-
key was the province of the *A Bicycle Culture*
pretentious or the British.

IN THE BRILLIANT SUN-
SHINE, THE RIMS AND SPOKES OF BICYCLE WHEELS
GLITTERED. The brightly colored jerseys of competitors contrasted with the green infield and fences as
they accelerated frenziedly. The metal roofs and
fences reverberated with shouts and stomping feet
of the spectators and the roar of their cheering was
deafening. In the large trees beyond the fences,
scores of desperate onlookers, too poor to purchase
tickets, hung from precarious perches peering
between and over the stands for a glimpse of the
contestants whizzing around the track.

Bicycle riding even now brings back Guyana
memories. For instance, as a teenager, I rode far out
of my way from school or after sports to pass the
home of a girl I loved madly. I knew what streets
she rode home from school or the houses of her
friends and I often "just happened" to pass her as
we cycled in opposite directions. Only a fleeting
sidelong glance acknowledged my presence but

seemed as wonderful as any conversation. I never did speak to her. When I was a little older and

Guyana Farewell more sophisticated, I contrived to ride alongside another girl I admired and ventured to rest my hand on hers as she held her bicycle handle. She told me that I was being fresh, but didn't disengage her hand immediately. Eventually, she even allowed me to tow her to a party on the crossbar of my bicycle – a thrill I never forgot.

Teen Parties

Dancing to popular music – whether doing
the "jump up" to the rhythms of calypso and steel
band or quick-stepping to tunes on radio or gramophone – was important to everyone in Guyana.
From early childhood, we twitched our shoulders
and shuffled our feet, wiggled our hips and bobbed
our heads in time to whatever was current in music.
Restricted in so many ways by the constraints of
our small society, our activities regulated by rules of
class, church, and government, our behavior inhib-
ited by Victorian concepts of morality, DANCING
PROVIDED A POWERFUL OUTLET FOR OUR ENERGY
AND SEXUALITY. All our celebrations – births and
birthdays, weddings and anniversaries, holidays and

festivals – were filled with dancing. We waltzed and tangoed, sambaed and rhumbaed, jitterbugged and jived, perspiring freely in the hot days and nights until our shirts and blouses clung damply to our shoulders and backs.

In our teens, we organized house parties on weekend evenings and holidays. Some parents, more indulgent than others, were persuaded to allow us to clear a living room for dancing. Someone's gramophone or record player was borrowed. Lists of girls and boys were carefully compiled and compared to ensure a reasonably equal balance. Certain attractive and popular girls were much in demand, although more emphasis was placed on conviviality and gaiety than popularity. It wasn't necessary to have a date. Girls brought food and boys paid a small admission fee. Everyone brought favorite records, which were heavy black disks in paper sleeves.

We jived and jitterbugged to Louis Armstrong and Glenn Miller, "jumped up" to the steel band records of Trinidadian groups, slow-danced to Billy Eckstine and Frank Sinatra, waltzed to Victor Sylvester, often until after midnight, restrained only

by the curfews established for girls. Tired, but
exhilarated, we then escorted the girls home. We

Guyana Farewell hoped for a quick kiss on the
doorstep or, better, a prolonged
session of necking. All the while
our ears were attuned to any door or window opening that might signal an irate, watching parent.

MY MOTHER WAS THE SCOURGE OF OUR
TEENAGE PARTIES. Because she prohibited us from
attending, we had to resort to countless sub-
terfuges. Stealing through the backdoor in the
darkness, shoes in hand, tiptoeing past loose boards
in the stairs, being careful to avoid rattling a bicycle
chain or causing any clatter of the footbridge out
of the yard, each of us, at different times, captivated
by the siren summons of dancing and flirtation,
escaped to the parties of friends.

My mother, rising from sleep, might accidentally discover our absence from our bed and, donning her clothes hurriedly, set out on her bike for
the most likely sites. These were the homes of those
friends whose parents she considered to be tolerant
of such sinful pastimes. In the quiet of our town,
the music from parties late at night was not diffi-

cult to hear. Mother would descend on some unsuspecting host with wrathful condemnation, seeking to seize her wayward child.

Teen Parties

All of our friends and, as our social circles widened as teenagers, many acquaintances, were aware of her predilection for such activity.

My mother's appearance outside a house where one of us might be gaily dancing would trigger an electric current of awareness and frantic warnings: *"Is Mrs. Bacchus outside!"* or, *"Oh, Lord! Is Sister V. downstairs! Run quick, mahn!"* Whichever of us it was would frantically exit through the back door or a window, climb over a back fence into a neighboring yard, reach home, take off our clothes, and lie panting in the darkness, listening for our mother's return as we feigned sleep. My mother's reluctance to disturb my father's rest was usually enough to ensure safety from immediate punishment, and the chances were good that by morning, preoccupied with her many activities, she might forget about the whole matter. My sister Sheila had the advantage of occasionally being permitted to stay over at my grandparents' house with my aunts,

Winnie and Edith. On those occasions, I imagined her dancing the night away at forbidden affairs.

Guyana Farewell   The prospect of being embarrassed by my mother's discovery and the mortifying accounts conveyed to me by close friends of my mother arriving unexpectedly and seizing my brother Ronald, were sufficient to dissuade me from such escapades. At least, sufficient until I fell in love and learned that the object of my affection was attending a party to which I was invited.

Knowing that my mother was at one of the periodic "revival" services of her church that evening, I set out for the party at a friend's house, "dressed to kill," as we often described a particularly notable effort in clothing. My guilt and apprehension about being discovered clashed with the sheer pleasure and delight of being close enough to touch, talk to and dance with this wonderful girl I had discovered. I was not so overwhelmed by the occasion that I did not cast occasional apprehensive glances out the window as it grew later and the chances of discovery heightened.

At midnight, with the lights low, dancing to a

slow tune, I looked up and, to my horror, saw
my mother's familiar face, hat firmly secured, in the

doorway of the house. I don't
remember disengaging or
what I mumbled but I have
rarely moved more quietly or
faster than that evening, slip-

Teen Parties

ping through the slow dancing couples, into the
kitchen past the startled faces of friends and down
the backsteps. I had had the prescience to leave
my bike next to the fence of an adjacent house. I
wheeled it quietly along the fences as far as the corner and without further ado, I MADE A RUNNING
JUMP, HIT THE SADDLE AND HEADED HOME HASTILY.
As I stole into the house and frantically donned
my pajamas, I heard my father mumble something
cautionary as I climbed into bed.

My wayward sense of humor, at just that
moment focused on the circumstances of my
abrupt abandonment of both partner and party,
seized me in a fit of giggles. My brother, David,
sleeping next to me, grumbled annoyedly as I
struggled to suppress the laughter that welled up
in me uncontrollably.

Movies &
Manners

Conforming to British custom, all cinemas were divided into differently priced sections of seats – orchestra, dress circle, balcony, and box. The section closest to the screen, the orchestra seats, was the cheapest and popularly referred to as "the pit." Presumably, this seating arrangement permitted patrons of all economic levels to afford the movies, thus allowing cinema owners and movie producers to widen their audiences substantially. It also reinforced the class distinctions that pervaded society, which essentially confined the poorest class to the lowest-priced sections, the upper middle class of civil service and commercial workers to the dress circle and allowed the pretentious, the rich or the

British to segregate themselves in the highest-priced seats.

Whatever the motives, this seating arrangement at cinemas resulted in the lowest-priced sections being considered off-limits to families, such as ours. The idea of being seen in the pit was anathema to us. Unless we could afford to pay dress circle prices, we were unlikely to go to the movies.

Escapades During the end-of-school-year holidays, from late July to early September, double features were offered at reduced prices in the early afternoon. These shows proved irresistible to my friends and me. AS TEENAGERS WITH LITTLE POCKET MONEY, WE WOULD BEG, BORROW OR STEAL THE FIFTEEN CENTS NEEDED FOR PIT SEATS. We pooled our funds and did whatever we could to raise enough to attend. Sometimes I might filch two or three of the coppers of change left by the maid for my mother after shopping. Our family friend Sister Jones was another source of finance, although it was important not to overdraw her generosity since her income from her market stall was quite low. We might accost the father of close friends of ours, Dr. Taitt, and prevail upon him to surrender a sixpence or two for the purpose. Occasionally, however, we would not have enough, and the person with

the lowest contribution would depart, dejectedly. To avoid being seen and identified by anyone in the dress circle, we purchased our tickets early and lingered furtively around the corner until the long, wooden shutters down the sides of the cinema began to be slammed shut by the attendants. Then, with heads lowered, WE SLIPPED QUICKLY INTO THE SEMI-DARKNESS, CHOOSING SEATS BELOW THE OVERHANGING SECTIONS OF THE DRESS CIRCLE. Mischievous friends or malicious acquaintances in the better sections and even in the pit might cry out loudly, amid jeering laughter:

"Eh, eh! Bacchus boy! Is dat you in the pit, deh? Ah see you sneakin' in!" Everyone laughed hysterically while the unfortunate one singled out cringed in embarrassment.

Despite the hard wooden benches and the malodorous ambiance of the pit, there was something magical about the transformation from the bright afternoon to the warm darkness of the cinema. Wherever you were sitting, when the attendants walked down the sides of the small wooden cinema, and began reaching up for the metal levers that controlled the tall shut- *Movies & Manners* ters in order to slam them shut, there was a feeling of fullness and expectancy. What a delicious feeling it was, sitting in the darkness watching the opening credits, secure from authority's watchful eye, shoulder to shoulder with friends, exclaiming with pleasure and wonder as the names of our favorite stars appeared on the screen.

One of my friends, Michael Branker, could never resist exclaiming rapturously when the name of one of his favorite film stars appeared on the screen.

"Oh, my dear me!," he would shout, *"My man, Bogie!"* or, *"Oh, rab, mahn! Is his lordship! Lord Humphie Bogart!"* We all groaned. We knew that for days afterward his ridiculous imitations of the gestures and speech of this particular idol would afflict all our conversations. He took to wearing a battered felt hat, spoke through carefully clenched lips and, when no adult was around, smoked cigarettes, which he held delicately between forefinger and thumb.

We lost ourselves in a fabulous world of make-believe, careening across the plains on galloping horses, crooning lullabies on Broadway to beautiful *Guyana Farewell* chorus girls, listening tight-lipped to briefings before manning our Spitfires, slipping surreptitiously down dark alleyways in Vienna, Berlin and Budapest and fencing madly up and down the stairs of castles and fortresses. What a world, what a time, what a life!

What a Show! My lifelong affair with the cinema had its roots in the circumstances that preceded my first movie; until I was about twelve years old, I had never seen a commercial movie. Like so many other treats enjoyed by my friends, movies were forbidden to me by my mother as a sinful indulgence. SHE SAW MOVIES AS THE FIRST STEP ON THE BROAD PATH TO HELL. The first time I went to a movie was one of the most fearful and wonderful experiences of my life.

I had been titillated and fascinated for years by the vivid descriptions of movies my friends saw. On Saturday afternoons, the absence of my friends signified their excursion to the movies, and I knew I would later be regaled and petrified by their ani-

mated accounts of *The Phantom of the Opera,*
The Mummy, The Hunchback of Notre Dame and

Frankenstein; tantalized and

shocked by visions of chorus
girls tapping and high-kick-
ing their way through *Stage
Door Canteen;* delighted and

mesmerized by descriptions of *Ali Baba, Sinbad* and
Tarzan of the Apes. The names of screen stars I had
never seen were a litany in my mind — an array of
vivid pictures in my imagination — Lon Chaney,
Turhan Bey, George Sanders, Greer Garson, Vivien
Leigh, Walter Pidgeon, Errol Flynn!

Passing the cinemas — the Empire, the Astor,
the Metropole — I would intently scrutinize the gar-
ish posters. Colorful and gaudy, they announced in
strident terms such films as *Waterloo Station, Mill
on the Floss, Mrs. Miniver, How Green Was My
Valley.* Particularly affecting were those at the
London Cincma across the street from my school
on Camp Street. Many were the afternoons I peered
longingly at the bright symbols and faces, dreaming
of their magical performances. For some reason, I
recall most clearly a wonderful poster advertising

Great Guns! starring Oliver and Hardy. Their
stunned faces, fingers crammed in their ears, next

Guyana Farewell
to cannons belching fire, is as
vivid now as it was then to that
thin little boy in short pants,

knees adorned with plasters, shirt hanging out,
standing in the still, hot afternoon, lost in contem-
plation of imagined escapades.

Finally, I screwed up my courage and, on
one of our annual bank holidays (which one I can't
recall), I took the plunge and sneaked off to the
Astor Cinema on Middle Street across from the
public hospital. I planned to see *The Adventures of
Robin Hood* – or was it *The Bandits of Sherwood
Forest* – with Erroll Flynn as Robin Hood.

I approached the ticket window with trepidation, carefully scrutinizing everyone in sight to
ascertain whether anyone knew me. In the bright-
ness of mid-afternoon, I felt cruelly exposed, certain that anyone could tell by looking at me that I
was doing something forbidden. I timed my entry
to the cinema just as the shutters were being closed,
so that there was still enough light for me to find a
seat in the unfamiliar place. I hoped fervently that

no one saw me sneaking into the movie.

My emotions were in turmoil as I sat in the dark intimacy of the pit, sur- *Movies & Manners* rounded by strangers, uncertain whether to stand for the playing of the British national anthem that preceded every public event. Conditioned since birth by adults to observe this ritual, I was shocked that most of those around me — obviously riff-raff — disdained to rise. Fearful of standing out, I REMAINED GLUED TO MY SEAT, ADDING ANOTHER TRANSGRESSION TO MY GUILT AND APPREHENSION. These conflicting emotions immediately vanished as the images appeared on the screen.

Enthralled, I watched the wonderful Looney Tunes, followed by the trailers of coming attractions. I was enveloped by the thrilling sound, the "Color by Technicolor," and my first sight on screen of some of the many famous names my friends had dunned into my brain over the years. With an enormous thrill, I saw the opening frames of the production; was it Metro-Goldwyn-Mayer with the ferocious, snarling lion's head or J. Arthur Rank's huge hammer swinging to strike a burnished shield with a resounding crash?

How avidly I perused the screen credits and
Guyana Farewell the names of the stars – Erroll
Flynn, Basil Rathbone and
others, followed by the names
of the producer and director! Then, with a sudden-
ness that stunned me, there appeared a cavalcade of
knights in glittering armor, their flags and pennants
fluttering, riding through a forest to the stentorian
sound of trumpets. Forever after, similar scenes in
cinemas in cities far distant from that warm, dusty
enclosure summon the sounds and smells, the thrill
and terror, and the wonder of my first experience of
the silver screen.

Vacations

School ended each year in July, and for four or five weeks we were free to enjoy ourselves. I remember those weeks most vividly in my pre-teen years when they seemed to stretch in wondrous, sun-filled emptiness. What stays with me most from those years is the annual trip we took to the country to spend a fortnight with church friends of my mother. The friends lived near Skeldon on the Corentyne River. Skeldon, Rose Hall, New Amsterdam, Rossignol – the names conjure vivid memories for me.

On the day of our departure, before dawn, stupid with sleep, we were bundled into the hired car for the trip to the station. The donkey cart had gone ahead an hour before with our luggage. At the station, finally awake, we scrambled for seats. My mother bullied the donkey cart man and the ragged porters into helping us find seats together. Tingling with excitement, we pushed and shoved and argued about window seats, peering out into the dawn as latecomers hurried to make the train. Finally, a blast of the conductor's whistle, a lurch and crunching of cars, a crescendo of cries, and the small, wooden train on its narrow-gauge tracks pulled out of the station.

As we gathered momentum slowly, the box-like cars with their slatted wooden seats swayed and rattled. WHAT A FEELING OF HAPPINESS AND WONDER AND ANTICIPATION SWEPT OVER US THEN! The locomotive belched black, sooty smoke that blew in the windows, sometimes smudging our clothes and sending cinders into our eyes. During infrequent lengthy stretches between stations when we summoned a good amount of speed, the rhythmic clacking of wheels on iron rails hypnotized us. We watched the sparks fly as we thundered over trestles, and caught glimpses of quiet creeks with empty punts, a bateau or a corial and a solitary paddler and vistas of rice, pale-green in the sunlight rising from watery, flooded fields. We stopped at

the open air wooden platforms of innumerable stations –

Buxton and Beterverwagting, Mahaica and Mahaicony, Cane Grove and Uitvlugt – stations filled with the bustle of passengers boarding with bundles and boxes, the cries of vendors offering fruits and sweets and snacks.

Once, on our way to Skeldon, we visited my father's relatives in a country village for a wedding celebration. Descendants of immigrants from India, these relatives maintained many of the customs and traditions of that far-off land. THE HOT AFTERNOON WAS FILLED WITH THE THROBBING OF DRUMS, THE ODD TUNELESS SINGING AND THE ULULATION AND WHINE OF UNFAMILIAR INSTRUMENTS. We were fussed over and cosseted, folded in the perfumed, ample bosoms of female relatives who were resplendent in colorful saris that yielded intriguing glimpses of naked waists and backs. Indulgent older men shook our hands and patted our heads while the children peered curiously at us.

The bride, who seemed not much older than

we were, was covered from head to foot in flowing white garments. In the bright sunshine silver glittered from her bracelets and bangles, her earrings and nose rings.

Food was served oudoors in the wide leaves of the banana plant to be eaten with one's fingers. Mounds of steaming white rice, pale yellow Madras mutton curries – lethal on the tongue – dahl, thick with lentils in thin calabashes, and sweet, sticky desserts of gulab jamun and jilaybee. We drank thirstily from pitchers of ice water and limeade while the perspiration beaded our foreheads and dripped on our garments. That afternoon still seems like a dream to me.

Continuing our journey the next day, we chugged and swayed past fields of sugar cane, the tall yellow and green shoots rising from the razor-edged leaves. We glimpsed the flash of cutlasses as half-naked brown and black laborers in ragged cutoffs and tattered headgear cleared and cut and stacked the bundles of sugar cane for loading on the punts. Iron punts, loaded high with the crop, moved sluggishly down the canals as the teams of

mules and bullocks on the beaten-down mud of
the towpaths strained and labored to pull them to
Guyana Farewell   the refineries. We imagined the
cries of the drivers and the snap
of the whips filling the air while
the bumping and grinding of the heavy punts sent
ominous warnings of crushed and broken limbs
to anyone careless in loading or stacking the crop.

In the late afternoon, our train reached
Rossignol on the Berbice River which was the end
of the line. We rushed to transfer our bags, suitcases
and bundles to the ferry where it waited, engines
throbbing, battered sides bumping against the huge
tires hanging from the sides of the stelling. THE
RIVER SEEMED THREATENING, DARK AS IT WAS WITH
SILT, SLOSHING AGAINST THE ENORMOUS PILINGS.
But in the distance on the other bank, we could
see the reassuring outlines of the houses of New
Amsterdam where we would spend the night at the
home of friends.

Early the next morning, we went to the bus
station, which was an open-air terminus filled with
rattletrap buses, engines belching and sputtering.
Here we embarked for Skeldon, our final destina-

tion. The garishly painted buses with their hard, slatted wooden seats were plastered with slogans: Never Say Die; Calypso King; *Vacations* Lord Invader. The roofs were stacked high with bundles and bags filled with produce and supplies. Women arrived, their heads swathed in colorful cloths, balancing large baskets and bundles, after walking several miles to get there. Hens and roosters and ducks, feet tied, were thrust unceremoniously under the seats, where they clucked and cackled and quacked with every bump of the buses.

All morning we careened down the dusty road, the bus clinging precariously to the two strips of cement laid down the width of a vehicle all along the single major road between the Berbice and Corentyne Rivers. Passing oncoming buses was a constant adventure. We would lurch sideways, the wheels on one side on gravel and those on the other on one concrete strip, and the passengers gesticulated in greeting or derision while the drivers blasted their horns enthusiastically and the livestock raised a din of protest.

Skeldon was a small village near the mouth of

the Corentyne River. The river constituted the boundary between the colonies of British and

Guyana Farewell

Dutch Guiana. The house of our friends, the Holders, was on the bank of the river, a little way from the village and a short walk from the highway. At this point, not far from where it flowed into the Atlantic, the Corentyne River was quite wide, with sandy beaches subject to the ebb and flow of the ocean tides. STONE JETTIES APPEARED AT INTERVALS, THRUSTING OUT INTO THE BROWN RIVER LIKE PALE RIBS.

Next door to the house was a small saw-mill where, in an enclosure adjoining the beach, untreated logs rested in piles like giant match sticks. On nights when it stormed and the tide was full, the logs heaved and rolled and ground against the fence, their gleaming surfaces momentarily revealed in the flare and wash of lightning, conveying a sense of crush and danger that seemed malignant and oppressive to our childish imaginations.

How to tell of the small terrors of childhood! The wizened, gray-bearded Indian man, naked except for his dhoti, walking along the beach with his head partially wrapped in a shabby cloth turban, somehow seemed threatening to us. The occasional stray dog hunched over stolen food, snarled possessively as we approached.

Vacations

Chiggers, tiny insects that burrowed into tender, bare soles, caused infection and had to be removed with a probing, insistent needle by my mother, who seemed impervious to our agonized screams as we writhed in her powerful and relentless grip. Mosquitoes hummed and whined after dark, hovering malevolently outside the mosquito nets to pounce on a limb carelessly thrust beyond the net. Occasionally, we were assaulted by an affliction of sand flies but, happily, this was infrequent.

Everything I recall from that trip seemed subject to the rhythmic rise and fall of the tides. We watched from the row of windows that overlooked the river as the first small ripples of water trembled past the ends of the jetty, slowly becoming a tidal surge until in an hour, perhaps, the waves splashed on the beach below and we could wade and swim and build channels to our castles in the sand.

At night when the tide was in, the waves created a susurration of sound that lulled us to sleep beneath our mosquito nets in our hammocks

Guyana Farewell   swinging gently to and fro. The sea air, soft, humid, languorous, smelling of shrimp and seashells, sawdust and seaweed, pressed like an invisible cover on our skinny, sleeping bodies.

Some mornings, I remember waking in the pre-dawn darkness, puzzled by the quiet, the absence of sea sounds, until a faint distant murmuring signaled that the tide was once more rising and soon the empty sand would be inundated.

Colophon

THE BACCHUS CHILDREN
(left to right)
Ronald, Sheila, David, Noël, Patrick
(Maxey not yet born)

COVER AND BOOK DESIGN
Derek Bacchus

EDITOR
Elizabeth Rogalin

TYPOGRAPHY
Garamond Roman and Italic, Künstler Script

PHOTOGRAPHY
Family archives, Derek Bacchus and
Carol Lee (p. 88; cover, top left & right)

PRINTED IN THE UNITED STATES OF AMERICA